SPECTRUM®

Reading

Grade 3

Published by Spectrum®
an imprint of Carson Dellosa Education
Greensboro, NC

Spectrum®
An imprint of Carson Dellosa Education
P.O. Box 35665
Greensboro, NC 27425 USA

ISBN 978-1-4838-1216-8

05-081217784

Table of Contents

Two Boys, Big Plans

Read to see what Sam and Kent are planning.

1 "Okay, I'm going to ask my parents right now. Are you?" Sam waited for Kent's reply over the phone.

2 "I think so," said Kent after a moment. "My dad just got home a little while ago. Are you bringing crackers?"

3 Sam laughed. Kent was always hungry. "Yes, I'll bring the crackers," he said. "And be sure to tell them that we'll turn the lights out by 9:30. Okay?"

4 "Nine-thirty. Right," Kent agreed. "Okay, I'm going to go ask. I'll talk to you in a little bit."

5 "Okay," answered Sam, and he hung up. *Now, if only we can talk our parents into letting us do this,* he thought to himself. He put on a big smile and entered the family room.

6 "Dad?" said Sam quietly so he wouldn't make his father jump. "I cleaned up those grass clippings for you."

7 "Oh, good," nodded Mr. Hume. "Thanks, Sam."

8 "Mom? Dad?" started Sam again. Both his parents looked over their newspapers. The words rushed out of Sam. "Kent and I were wondering if we could sleep out in the tent tonight. We'd be warm enough in our sleeping bags, and we won't eat too much, and it'll be lights out at 9:30, we promise."

9 Mr. and Mrs. Hume blinked, then looked at each other. *How do they talk to each other without saying anything?* wondered Sam.

10 "Did Kent's parents say it was okay?" asked Mrs. Hume.

11 "He's asking right now." Sam shifted from one foot to the other. Another look passed between his parents.

12 Mr. Hume nodded. "If Kent's parents say it's okay, it's okay with us."

13 "Thanks, Dad! Thanks, Mom!" called Sam as he dashed for the phone. He dialed and held his breath. Then, he heard Kent's voice.

14 "Okay?" asked Sam.

15 "Okay!" said Kent.

NAME ______________________________

1. This story is mostly about
   ______ a sleepover.
   ______ Sam's parents.
   __✓__ two boys' plans.

2. At the beginning, when Sam and Kent are talking on the phone, what did you think they might be talking about?

   ____

   ____

3. In the story, when did you find out what the boys are planning?

   ____

4. Why do you think Sam told his dad about the grass clippings?

   ____

   ____

5. Why does Sam mention being warm enough and when the lights will be turned out?

   ____

   ____

6. Now that the boys have permission, what do you think they will do next?

   ____

   ____

7. In paragraph 5, why are the words *Now, if we can only talk our parents into letting us do this* in italics?

   ____

8. What is the author's purpose in writing this selection?

   ____

9. Have you ever been worried about asking your parents to do something? What was it, and how did you ask them?

   ____

   ____

One Tent, Lots of Stuff

What do the boys need for their night in the tent?

1 "Lantern?"

2 "Got it."

3 "Sleeping bags?"

4 "Got it—both of them."

5 "Pillows?"

6 "Two fat ones."

7 "Crackers?"

8 "Three kinds."

9 "Three kinds? Great!"

10 Sam and Kent had made a list of all the things they needed for sleeping out in the tent. Now, they were sitting cross-legged in the tent, checking things off the list.

11 "Are you going to bring a bathrobe and slippers?" Kent asked Sam.

12 "Oh, no! We're camping. Those are just for in the house," answered Sam, looking as if he knew all about camping.

13 "Oh, right," said Kent, who had never been camping before. He didn't think Sam had been camping before either. Still, it was Sam's dad's tent, so he must know.

14 "Oh, I almost forgot. Can you bring your baseball glove?" Sam looked very serious.

15 Kent couldn't figure this one out. "My baseball glove? What do we need that for?"

16 "Well, we just might. You never know," said Sam with mystery and authority.

17 "Okay," shrugged Kent, "I'll bring it when I come after supper. What time do you think you'll be able to come out?"

18 Sam thought for a moment. "We usually eat at 5:45. Then, I have to clear the table. I should be done by 6:30. What about you?"

19 "My dad doesn't get home until six o'clock," said Kent, regretfully. "Maybe if I offer to help Mom with supper, things will go quickly."

20 Sam shrugged. "It's worth a try. Come out as soon as you can." Sam looked around the tent. "Okay, I think everything's ready. I'll see you later."

21 "See you later," said Kent, and the boys both ran home.

NAME ______________________

1. One of the boys usually has the ideas. The other one seems to go along with those ideas. Which boy is the "leader"?

____

2. What details from the story helped you answer question 1?

____

____

3. Kent says he might help his mom with supper. What does that tell you about Kent?

____

4. Based on what you know about camping, how do you feel about all the stuff the boys have in their tent? List what you think they need and what they don't need.

What They Need

____

What They Don't Need

____

5. In some stories, the author tells you what is happening. In this story, the author uses mostly dialogue, what the characters say, to let you know what is going on. Choose one line of dialogue and write what it helps you know about the character.

Dialogue: ______________________

____

____

6. Why does Kent think that Sam knows more about camping?

____

____

7. How do you think the boys feel about camping out together? Explain your answer.

____

____

How to Pitch a Tent

Follow these instructions to learn how to pitch a tent.

These general instructions should allow anyone to pitch any size or style of tent. Keep in mind that pitching a tent alone, even if you have experience, is difficult.

1. Choose a flat area on which to pitch your tent. Remove any stones or rocks that might poke through the tent's floor.
2. Take the tent and all equipment out of the storage bag. Lay everything on the ground neatly.
3. Spread a groundcloth over the chosen spot. Then, lay the tent floor over the groundcloth. Fold the edges of the groundcloth under, so they do not stick out from the edges of the tent.

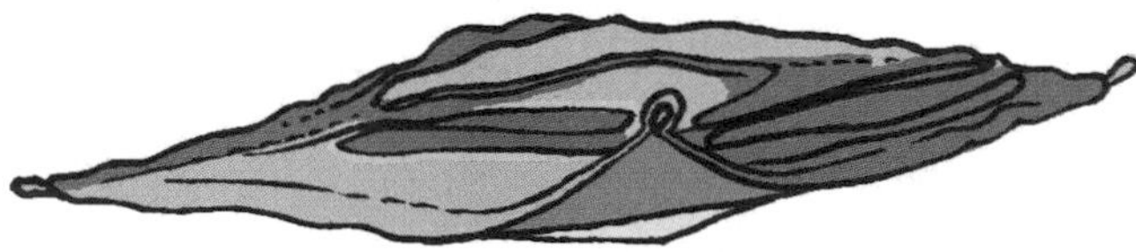

4. Make sure the tent door is zipped shut. Then, pound a stake through each loop, pulling snugly as you go so the floor gets stretched to its full size.

5. Put together the tent poles, if necessary. Thread each one through its loops or channels. Do not step or walk on the tent to do this. If necessary, crawl or lie down on your stomach to reach the center of the tent.

6. Raise the poles. If you have a partner, work on opposite sides of the tent.

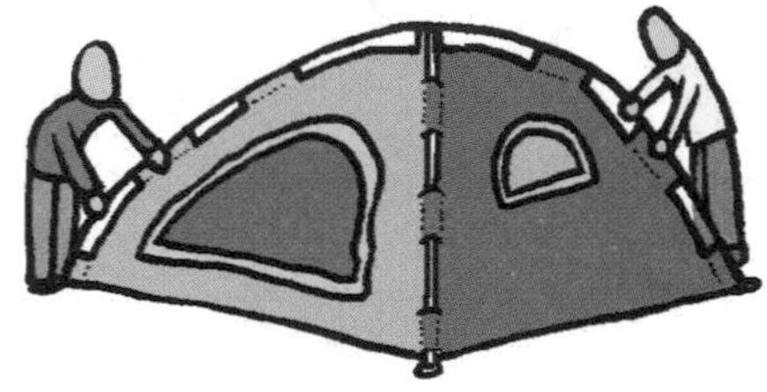

7. Pull the guy lines straight out from the sides of the tent. Peg each one.

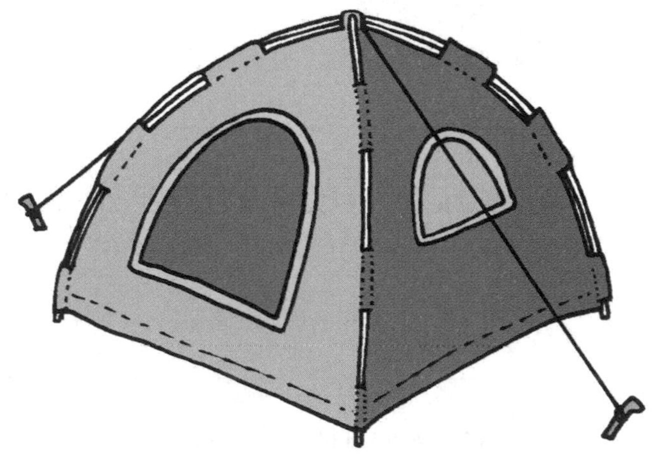

NAME ______________________________

1. What do you know about pitching a tent? Do you have anything to add to these instructions?

____

____

2. Number the sentences to show the order of steps to pitch a tent.
   ______ Spread out groundcloth.
   ______ Tighten and peg guy lines.
   ______ Choose and clear an area.
   ______ Put together tent poles.
   ______ Lay out equipment.
   ______ Pound stakes through loops.
   ______ Raise the poles.

3. If you don't know or understand what a guy line is, which illustration helps you figure it out? Tell how.

____

____

4. Choose one illustration. Explain what it shows.

____

____

____

5. In the first paragraph, the author says that pitching a tent alone is difficult. Why do you think this is?

____

____

6. What is the purpose of a groundcloth?

____

7. Which two steps explain what to do with the poles?

______________________ and ______________________

8. After reading these instructions, do you think you could pitch a tent? Why or why not?

____

____

One Tent...What Next?

What do the boys expect to happen?

1 "Then, there was the time my brother and I nearly got blown away with the tent! Did I tell you about that one?" Sam shook his head and tried not to look impatient. His dad had been telling camping stories for almost an hour. *How can I get him to stop without saying anything?* thought Sam to himself. He really wanted to get out to the tent.

2 Finally, his dad stopped for a bite of dessert, and Sam asked to be excused. When his mom nodded her head okay, it took only four trips to clear the table. Then, he was off and across the backyard.

3 "Caught you!" yelled Sam as he flipped back the tent flap. Kent jumped and turned red. "Ha! I knew it! In the crackers already." Then, he laughed. "Have you been waiting long?"

4 Kent shook his head because his mouth was full. Finally, he said, "Not long. My dad got home late."

5 Sam shrugged. "Oh, well. We're here now. Let's get ready."

6 "Ready for what?" asked Kent.

7 "For whatever's going to happen," answered Sam. *Well, he must know,* thought Kent. He helped Sam straighten the sleeping bags and stash stuff in the corners. They played catch across the tent for a little while. *Ah, the baseball glove,* thought Kent. They played badminton with crackers, but then Sam discovered crumbs in his sleeping bag, so they stopped.

8 They turned on the lantern and read. After a while, Sam retold some of his dad's camping stories. Then, Kent turned out the light, and they listened for noises in the dark. They didn't hear any for a very long time.

9 Finally, Kent heard something at the tent flap. He half crawled and half flew across the tent to warn Sam. Sam yelled when Kent landed on top of him.

10 "Hey, are you guys all right?" It was Sam's mom. "Breakfast is ready."

11 Sam and Kent looked at each other in disbelief. They had slept through the whole night, and nothing had happened.

NAME ______________________________

1. Which sentence best describes this story?
   ______ Nothing exciting happens to the boys in the tent.
   ______ The boys have a crazy night in the tent.
   ______ In the morning, Kent plays a trick on Sam and scares him.

2. Why did the boys stop playing badminton?

   ____

   ____

3. Read the sentences below. Write **F** next to sentences that are facts and **O** next to sentences that are opinions.
   ______ Kent eats too many crackers.
   ______ Sam's dad had been telling camping stories for almost an hour.
   ______ Breakfast is ready.
   ______ Sam's dad tells the best camping stories.

4. What do you think the boys were hoping would happen?

   ____

   ____

   ____

5. In paragraph 3, why does Kent turn red?

   ____

   ____

6. Write **C** next to the sentence below that is the cause. Write **E** next to the sentence that is the effect.
   ______ Kent landed on top of Sam.
   ______ Sam's mom startled the boys.

7. This story has two settings. What are they?

   ____________________________ and ____________________________

Night Lights

What is keeping Mikki awake?

1 There were lights flashing outside. No matter what I did, I could see those lights. I couldn't figure out what they were, so I started worrying.

2 I turned away from the window and closed my eyes. But then I had to open them, just a crack, to see if the lights were still there. *Flash-flash, off, flash!*

3 I rolled toward the window and watched. Maybe I could figure it out. I started listing things. Car lights? Not bright enough. Police car flashers? Not blue and red enough. Spaceships? Not likely. All right, this is really bugging me. I have to go ask Mom, I finally concluded.

4 I padded downstairs where my mom was reading a magazine. She was a little surprised to see me.

5 "The lights are flashing upstairs," I said.

6 "They are?" She said it with that "this is a great excuse for being out of bed" look on her face.

7 "I can't figure out what it is," I continued, hoping for some comfort. To my relief, she put down her magazine and steered me back upstairs.

8 We laid across my bed on our stomachs and watched out the window. Mom knew right away.

9 "Mikki, do you remember driving up to visit Uncle Walt last month?" she asked. I nodded. "Do you remember how long it took?" I nodded again. "Well, Uncle Walt is having a thunderstorm way up north where his house is. The lightning is sort of shining off the clouds, so we can see the flashing down here, even though the storm is far away from us."

10 "Oh," I said. I thought to myself, *Well, that makes sense.* After all, what else causes lights to flash in the sky? Aliens? Not likely.

NAME ______________________________

1. What is causing Mikki to worry?

____

2. What does Mikki do to try to get to sleep?

First, she ______________________________________

____

Then, she ______________________________________

____

3. What is causing the flashing lights?

____

____

4. Have you ever been kept awake at night by something that bothered or puzzled you? Write about it.

____

____

____

5. From whose point of view is this story told?

______ Mom's ______ Mikki's ______ Uncle Walt's

6. Which word best describes Mom in the story?

______ impatient ______ confused ______ kind

7. Is this story realistic? Why or why not?

____

____

8. Name three things that Mikki thinks the lights could be.

______________ ______________ ______________

Thunder and Lightning

What causes thunder and lightning?

1 The story of thunder and lightning is a lesson on electricity. Lightning is really just a giant electrical spark. Thunder is a direct result of the activity of that spark.

Lightning First

2 Imagine a single water droplet high above Earth. It is in a cloud among millions of other water droplets. As this water droplet falls toward Earth, it gets bigger by collecting more moisture. When the droplet gets to just about the size of a pea, it splits. This splitting action causes an electrical charge to build up on the two new droplets.

3 If the droplets fall straight to Earth, the electrical charge is very small and will have no effect. If the droplets get swept upward by air currents, however, the whole process begins again. The droplets fall, grow, split, and become more strongly charged with electricity each time.

4 In time, the electrical charge in the droplets becomes so strong that it has to discharge itself. The result is a huge spark. It may leap from a cloud to the ground in less than one-tenth of a second. We know it as lightning.

Thunder Second

5 When lightning flashes, the air is suddenly heated, and then it quickly cools. These rapid changes in the air cause the cracking sound of thunder. During a storm, we see lightning first, and then wait to hear the thunder. That's because light travels faster than sound. We see the lightning as it happens, but the sound of the thunder may take any number of seconds to reach us, depending on how far away the lightning was. The rumbling sound of thunder is actually an echo from the sound waves bouncing off Earth or off the clouds.

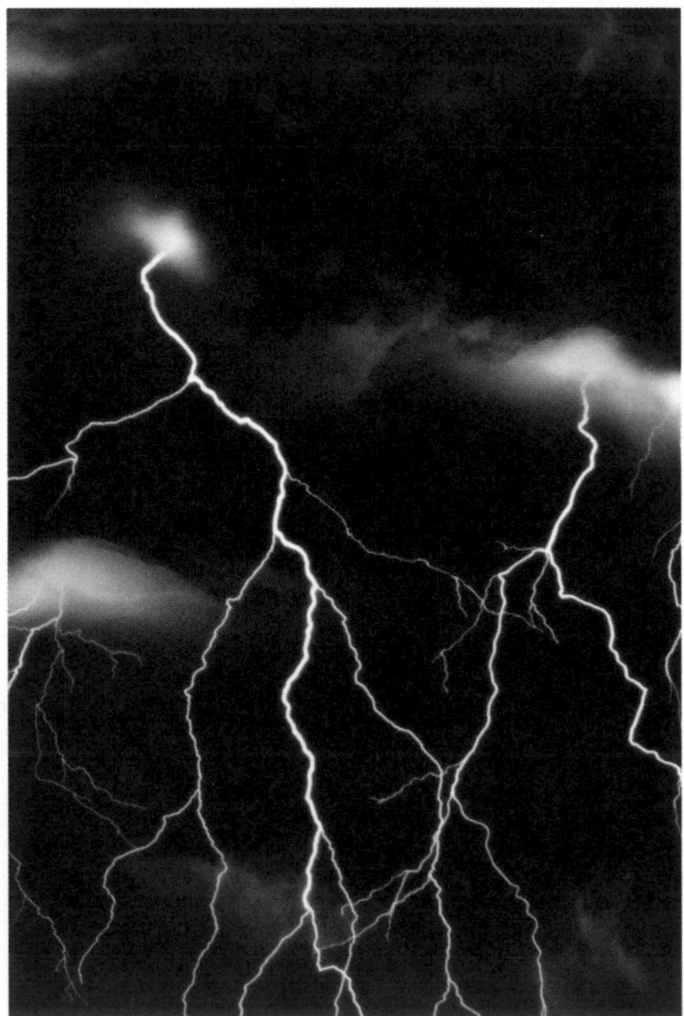

NAME ______________________________

1. The author wrote this article to
   ______ entertain.
   ______ give information.
   ______ persuade.

2. Which comes first, thunder or lightning?

   ____

3. What causes lightning? Give a brief answer.

   ____

   ____

   ____

4. How does lightning cause thunder?

   ____

   ____

   ____

5. If you read only the two headings in this article, what would you learn?

   ____

   ____

   ____

6. Write **T** for true or **F** for false next to each statement below.
   ______ Thunder always takes the same amount of time to reach Earth.
   ______ Light travels faster than sound.
   ______ Thunder and lightning are not related to each other.

7. What is the main idea of paragraph 4?

   ____

   ____

   ____

8. Which of the following is the purpose of paragraph 1?
   ______ introduction ______ author's purpose ______ conclusion

Smokey the Bear

Read to find out how Smokey the Bear became famous.

1 Smokey the Bear's story doesn't start with a bear. It starts with a problem, a solution, and then a drawing.

2 In the 1940s, during World War II, the leaders of the United States had a problem. They were worried about having enough wood to build ships and other equipment for the war. The solution: To protect America's forests (and the wood that might be needed for ships), the U.S. Forest Service started a campaign to prevent forest fires.

3 The Forest Service created posters reminding people about fire safety. The posters featured a deer named Bambi from a popular movie. Before long, however, the poster images were switched to a popular toy animal—a bear. An illustrator, Albert Staehle, drew that first bear with a park ranger's hat in 1944 and named him *Smokey*.

4 Six years later, while fighting a forest fire in New Mexico, firefighters found a black bear cub clinging to a tree. They rescued the cub and called it Hotfoot. Soon, however, the cub was renamed Smokey after the drawings on the posters.

5 Once he recovered from his injuries, Smokey was taken to the National Zoo in Washington, D.C. Thousands of people visited him there until he died in 1976. Smokey was 26 years old. His message is still with us, however, as we see him reminding us to prevent forest fires all across the nation.

NAME ______________________

Put a check next to the sentences that are true.

1. ______ The idea for Smokey the Bear started in the 1940s.
2. ______ Smokey the Bear lives in New Mexico.
3. ______ The Forest Service made posters in honor of a bear cub that died in a fire.
4. ______ Smokey the Bear was a drawing first, and then a real bear.

Write **M** next to the sentences that tell about make-believe things.

5. ______ Smokey the Bear lived in a zoo for many years.
6. ______ Smokey the Bear speaks to campers about the danger of forest fires.
7. ______ Smokey the Bear used to help firefighters put out fires.
8. Why was Smokey the Bear created? Write the phrase or sentence from the article that tells you.

   ____

   ____

   ____

9. In paragraph 2, what problem did U.S. leaders have?

   ____

10. What was the solution?

    ____

11. What organization created the fire safety posters?

    ____

12. In the posters, did Smokey the Bear look realistic? Explain.

    ____

    ____

Planting Dreams

What does Rosa dream about?

1 She was walking home from work one evening when she got the idea. Rosa didn't like her job at the factory, but it was better than no job at all. So, while she was trying not to think about work, she saw the pots stacked up in an alley. They were cheap plastic pots, but there were dozens of them piled up behind the flower shop. *Such a waste,* she thought. When the pots were still there three days later, Rosa went in and asked if she could take some. The flower shop lady said she didn't mind, so Rosa carried home a tower of pots, pretending she was a circus performer on the way.

2 At home, Rosa set the pots on the fire escape outside her tiny apartment. And there they sat. Once, a gust of wind sent them clattering to the street three floors below, and she had to go and chase them before the gathering storm.

3 Every day, Rosa went to work and thought about her pots. She was waiting for something, but she had patience.

4 At last, the newspaper brought good news. A hardware store had a sale on potting soil. Rosa carefully counted her money, and then she walked the six blocks to the store. She bought six bags and carried them home. She bought seeds, too. Rosa slept well that night and dreamed of masses of flowers and fat, glowing fruits.

5 Sundays were always good days. Rosa didn't have to work on Sundays. But Rosa couldn't remember when she had had *such* a good Sunday. She got up early and ate her breakfast on the fire escape with her pots. Then, she began to scoop dirt into the pots. She hummed a little song until all six of her bags of soil were empty. Then, she laid her precious seed packets out and planned her garden. Tomatoes for the biggest pots, and peppers for the next-biggest ones. Flowers in all the rest.

6 At the end of the day, Rosa sat in her garden and watched the sunset. *Soon,* she thought, *there will be masses of flowers and fat, glowing fruits.*

NAME ______________________

A **fact** is something that can be proven true. An **opinion** is what someone thinks or feels. Check the sentences that are facts.

1. ______ Vegetables can be grown in pots.
2. ______ Creating a garden on a fire escape is difficult.
3. ______ Any garden is beautiful.
4. ______ Plants need soil and water.
5. Number the sentences to show the order in which things happened.
   ______ Rosa bought potting soil.
   ______ Rosa took the pots home.
   ______ Rosa planted her seeds.
   ______ Rosa saw the pots.
6. Check the words or phrases that best describe Rosa.
   ______ selfish
   ______ tends to waste time
   ______ likes the outdoors
   ______ appreciates beauty
7. Why do you think Rosa slept well the night after she bought seeds and soil?
   ____
   ____
   ____
8. The author repeats a line from paragraph 4 in the last paragraph. What line is it? Why do you think the author repeats it?
   ____
   ____
   ____
9. Have you ever planted something and watched it grow? Tell about how it made you feel.
   ____
   ____
   ____
   ____

Dreaming of the Harvest

Read to see how Rosa's garden is doing.

1 Rosa hurried home from work. She knew it had been quite warm that day, and it hadn't rained since last week. She was worried that her tiny seedlings might have gotten too much sun. When she got to her building, she raced up the stairs, two at a time, up to the third floor.

2 Rosa was still panting when she stepped out onto the fire escape. *Oh, you poor things!* was all she could think. Even her strongest, tallest tomato plant looked as if it had just given up. It was pale and dry looking, not green and smooth like it had been this morning. Rosa got her watering can and went right to work. She watered each pot until it began to drip out the holes in the bottom. She made sure each plant got just the right amount. Then, she went in to fix something to eat.

3 In the kitchen, Rosa bit into an apple and imagined that it was a big, juicy tomato. She chopped a carrot and imagined that it was a shiny, green pepper getting ready to join some tomatoes in a pot of rich, spicy sauce.

4 She carried her dinner out to the fire escape. The apartment building across the street cast its shadow on her garden, letting it rest from the day's hot sun. Rosa leaned against the wall and closed her eyes. She let her hard day of work at the factory fade away as she imagined taking her flowers to her friends at work. Just think how surprised they would be. They would think she had robbed the flower shop!

5 Rosa watched her garden grow until after dark. Then, she went inside and dreamed of running her own shop filled with trays of fresh vegetables and baskets of flowers fresh from her own garden.

NAME ______________________________

1. Why is Rosa worried about her plants on this day?

____

____

Write **T** if the sentence is true. Write **F** if the sentence is false.

2. ______ This story is mostly about Rosa worrying about her garden.
3. ______ Rosa is careless about her garden.
4. ______ Rosa plans to share her flowers with others.
5. ______ Too much sun causes Rosa's plants to dry up.

Compare how things really are with how they used to be, or with what Rosa imagines.

6. The strongest, tallest tomato plant is ______________________________.
   It had been ______________________________.
7. Rosa bites into an ______________________________.
   She imagines that it is a ______________________________.
8. She chops a ______________________________.
   She imagines that it is a ______________________________.
9. For now, Rosa works at a ______________________________.
   She dreams of ______________________________.
10. Why do you think Rosa spends so much time daydreaming?

____

____

11. What details from the story helped you answer question 10?

____

____

12. Which of these is mostly likely to be true?
    ______ Rosa lives in the country.
    ______ Rosa lives in a city.

Peppers

Which kind of pepper do you like best?

1 What comes in many colors and is high in vitamins A and C? Some people like them hot; some prefer them mild. They are a common sight in backyard gardens throughout the United States. Have you guessed yet? They are peppers.

2 Whether green, yellow, or red, peppers add flavor to many types of foods. People eat them raw, pickled, or cooked. They go in salads, in sauces, on sandwiches, and, of course, on pizza.

Bell Peppers

3 The mildest variety of pepper is the bell pepper. They are sometimes called *sweet peppers,* but they are not sweet like sugar. They are simply less spicy, or hot, than other types of peppers. The round, apple-sized fruits of bell pepper plants are green, yellow, or red. Some people eat them before they get fully ripe. Bell peppers are by far the most common pepper found in gardens and on grocery store shelves.

Chili Peppers

4 "Chili pepper" is a general name for a number of quite spicy peppers that come in many sizes and appear red, yellow, or green. These hotter peppers tend to be long and skinny. Chili peppers don't actually burn your mouth, but they can cause pain. A certain chemical in the fruit causes this feeling. Chili peppers, whether fresh or dried, add an almost fiery zing to foods. Dishes from Mexico, India, and Africa are noted for including the hottest types of peppers. Eating these foods may take some getting used to. In addition to the discomfort in your mouth, hot peppers may cause your eyes to water, your nose to run, and your ears to feel warm.

5 Whatever their color or flavor, peppers add variety and spice to fancy or even everyday foods. When was the last time you had a pepper?

NAME ______________________

1. What do you know about peppers, or what experiences have you had growing or eating peppers?

____

____

2. Do you like peppers? Write why or why not.

____

3. How are bell peppers and chili peppers the same? How are they different? Write what the article tells you about each kind.

Bell Peppers

Size ______________

Shape ______________

Color ______________

Flavor ______________

Chili Peppers

Size ______________

Shape ______________

Color ______________

Flavor ______________

4. What two headings does the author divide the article into? How is this helpful?

____

____

5. Write **T** for true or **F** for false next to each statement below.

______ Hot peppers can make your eyes water.

______ Bell peppers are very spicy.

______ Peppers can be prepared in many ways.

______ Bell peppers are red, and chili peppers are green.

6. What makes chili peppers burn your mouth?

____

7. What two vitamins are peppers high in?

______________ and ______________

The Pie Man

Read to see what Mr. Fellini remembers about his career.

1 Joseph Fellini waited for the light to change. Even early in the morning, Central Park South was busy and noisy. He knew that just across the street in the park, it would be quiet and pleasant. *Some things don't change,* he thought with a sigh.

2 When Joseph was a young man, people didn't realize how important it was to go to college. All that Joseph had wanted at age 17 was to get a job to help make sure he and his parents had food to eat. Food was what steered him to the bakery, he figured. It always smelled so good. He walked three blocks out of his way on the way home from high school just to smell it. Then, one May day, there was a sign on the door.

Wanted:
Delivery Driver
Inquire Within

3 Right after he graduated, Joseph became Mr. Fellini, the "Pie Man." His work day started at 5 A.M. The bakers had already been at work for hours, putting together apple, cherry, peach, chocolate custard, banana cream, and all kinds of other pies. When Joseph arrived, the pies were in boxes and lined up on trays, ready for him to put into his truck. Joseph had always loved the smell of all those fresh pies, mingled and warm in the back of his truck. He never tired of that smell, even after 53 years on the job.

4 When Joseph was out in his truck, he felt important. The people who worked at the restaurants where he delivered the pies were always glad to see him. Out in traffic, people would sometimes make way for the Pie Man. They knew he had special cargo that needed to be delivered safe and fresh.

5 As Joseph strolled along Central Park West, he saw a pie truck. The young man at the wheel was beeping his horn impatiently. *Ah,* thought Joseph, *slow down. You still have 52 years to go.*

NAME ____________________

1. What was Joseph's main goal in getting a job at 17?

2. Why did Joseph always make a point to walk past the bakery?

3. Who started work earlier, Joseph or the pie bakers?

4. Who is the main character in this story?

5. Would you describe young Joseph as serious or dreamy? Write why.

6. How did Joseph feel about his job?

7. Do you think Joseph was a good worker? Explain.

8. Do you think Joseph has lived in the same city his whole life? Explain.

9. At the end of the story, how does Joseph feel when he sees a young pie man act impatiently?

Once a Pie Man, Always a Pie Man

What does Mr. Fellini do now that he doesn't deliver pies?

1 *Which way shall I go today?* Joseph thought to himself as the signs pointed this way and that. *I think Turtle Pond needs a visitor,* he decided. He followed the path to the right, toward the middle of Central Park. Around a curve, he had to step off the sidewalk as a line of mothers and baby strollers marched by. They didn't walk, they marched. Joseph had heard it called *power walking. I suppose it's good for them,* he thought, shaking his head. But he also thought their marching didn't allow them to notice the birds or the flowers.

2 At Turtle Pond, two young children had spied a turtle. It must have been their first one, judging by their excitement. Joseph smiled as he watched. He could remember being that excited about turtles when he was young.

3 From Turtle Pond, it was an easy walk to the art museum. Joseph sat down on a bench in the sun. He liked to watch all the different kinds of people go to the art museum. In a way, he thought the people were just like the pieces of art. Each one looked different and had a different reason for being there.

4 When he had soaked up enough sun, Joseph wandered toward Cedar Hill, then out to Fifth Avenue. A quick check of his watch told him he was right on time.

5 A pie truck pulled up.

6 "What'll it be today, Mr. Fellini?" said the young driver.

7 Joseph thought for a moment. "I think today is a peach day, Mr. Tarentino."

8 "Peach it is, Mr. Fellini," and the young man swung out of his seat and disappeared into the back of his truck. Behind the truck, cars waited, the drivers oddly patient. They knew the Pie Man had important business.

NAME ______________________________

1. As you began to read about Mr. Fellini's walk in the park, what did you think was going to happen?

____

____

2. Predict what Mr. Fellini will do next.

____

3. Which of these does Mr. Fellini see on his walk?
   ______ a work of art
   ______ children and turtles
   ______ mothers and baby strollers
   ______ a nest of young birds

4. Which of these best describes Mr. Fellini?
   ______ thoughtful ______ anxious ______ impatient

5. Reread the last two lines of paragraph 8. Why is it odd that the cars waited patiently?

____

____

6. Why does Mr. Fellini think that the power-walking mothers should slow down?

____

____

7. Write **C** next to the sentence below that is the cause. Write **E** next to the sentence that is the effect.

   ______ A line of mothers and baby strollers marched by.

   ______ Mr. Fellini had to step off the sidewalk.

8. Give an example of a line of dialogue from the story.

____

____

9. Mr. Fellini appreciates the small things in life. Do you agree or disagree? Why?

____

____

New York City's Gem

Find out what there is to see and do in Central Park.

1 It has been called "a wonder" and "an oasis." People go there to exercise or to relax. It is included on almost every tour of New York City because of its beauty. It is neither a historic building nor a skyscraper. It is Central Park.

2 Lying in the heart of Manhattan, Central Park is still the green space that its founders hoped it would be. As the city's population grew rapidly in the early 1800s, a few wise men saw the need to set aside some space that would give residents a break from the crowded city's hurry and noise.

3 The park's plan, developed in 1858, was a daring one. The chosen land was rocky, swampy, and muddy. For these reasons, the area was completely transformed in a project that took 20 years. Top soil from New Jersey came in horse-drawn carts. Lakes were dug. Boulders were blasted out, then carted away. Four million trees, shrubs, and plants were carted in and planted.

4 Though its appearance has changed during the last 150 years, Central Park continues to be an important place for tourists and New Yorkers alike.

Central Park by the Numbers

25,000,000	Number of visitors to Central Park each year
26,000	Number of trees growing in Central Park
8,968	Number of benches in Central Park
843	Total acres of Central Park
275	Different types of birds found in Central Park
250	Number of acres of lawn in Central Park
150	Number of acres covered by water in Central Park
136	Number of wooded acres in Central Park
58	Total miles of walking paths in Central Park
6	Distance, in miles, around outside edge of Central Park

NAME ______________________

1. The article contains a feature box titled "Central Park by the Numbers." What kind of information is in the box?

____

____

2. Why do you think this information was shown in a separate list instead of in the text?

____

____

3. When was Central Park planned?

____

4. The park was a daring project because

____

______________________.

5. If you walked on all of the walking paths in the park, you would walk

____

6. Which is greater, the number of trees or the number of benches?

____

7. For what reason was Central Park created?

____

____

8. How is Central Park different from an average city park?

____

____

9. Have you ever visited Central Park? If you have, tell what it was like. If you haven't, tell what you might like to do there.

____

____

____

Soccer Blues

Why is Perry so unhappy about soccer practice?

1 "Okay, everybody, come over here and listen up!" Coach's voice carried across the soccer field. Kids of all sizes and shapes stopped what they were doing and walked or trotted toward the coach. When the several dozen boys and girls were in a ring around him, the coach continued. "I want all of you to practice dribbling on your own for at least half an hour a day outside of practice. Okay?"

2 "Okay, Coach!" yelled the circle. Everyone smiled. Coach always liked answers to his questions.

3 Satisfied with the response, Coach went on. "Most of the passing we do in games is when we're only 10, maybe 20, yards apart. We need to be able to deliver the ball within that range *every time we pass,*" Coach explained. "Now, we're going to do a one-on-one passing exercise. One partner over here, the other over there," he said, pointing to one touch line and another invisible line about half-way across the field. "What I want you to do is...."

4 Around the circle, heads nodded as eager players listened to Coach. One head, though, wasn't nodding; it was bobbing. Perry was so tired and hungry that his knees felt shaky. He was sure he had dribbled his soccer ball a hundred miles already this afternoon. He felt as if one more passing exercise would pretty much finish him off. Somehow, he stumbled through. He was pretty sure he did not impress Coach, though, when one of his passes went wildly across the field.

5 At the end of practice, Perry flopped into the back seat of the car and buckled his seatbelt. He didn't even wait for his mom's usual question.

6 "Practice was awful," said Perry without even opening his eyes. "I don't ever want to go back."

NAME ______________________

1. In most stories, a character has a problem. What is Perry's problem?

____

2. What information in the story helped you answer question 1?

____

____

3. **Dialogue** is what the characters in a story say. What did you learn about Perry from his dialogue?

____

____

4. Find a line of the coach's dialogue. What does it tell you about the coach?

   Dialogue: ______________________

   ____

   What it tells: ______________________

   ____

5. Coach thinks that a passing exercise is important because

____

______________________.

6. What is the setting for this story?

____

7. **Practice was awful.** Is this a fact or an opinion?

____

8. The last line of paragraph 5 says that Perry didn't even wait for his mom's usual question. What do you think her question is?

____

9. Which word or phrase best describes Perry in this story?

   ______ confident ______ full of energy ______ exhausted

10. Have you ever wished you could quit an activity? Tell about it.

____

____

Mom to the Rescue

Have you ever solved a mystery?

1 Mrs. Rothman was speechless. The only thing Perry had talked about all winter was soccer. Now, Perry wanted to quit soccer. Not knowing whether to laugh or cry, she drove home and fixed dinner.

2 After dinner, Mrs. Rothman tried to get to the bottom of the problem.

3 "Do you think Coach is too tough?"

4 "No."

5 "Are you having trouble with one of the other kids?"

6 "No."

7 "Did you get hurt?"

8 "No."

9 "Do you feel as if you're not good enough? If that's the case, you should talk to Coach...."

10 "Well, that's sort of it. I just felt so weak during practice. My knees were shaky. I could hardly lift my feet." Perry shook his head. "I just don't have what it takes. A soccer player has to run and run and not even get winded."

11 *Hmm,* thought Mrs. Rothman. *Weak? Shaky knees?* She softened her questioning a little. "Did you have a good lunch today?"

12 Perry thought for a second. "Um, yes, I guess so. Oh, except that there was a fire drill, and I didn't get to finish."

13 *Aha, that's it! A boy can't make it through school and soccer practice without the proper fuel.*

14 "I'll tell you what, Perry," said Mrs. Rothman, patting his knee. "Why don't you try it for one more day. I'll meet you after school with a power snack, and we'll see if that helps." Perry agreed, but he wondered what a power snack was and how it could possibly help.

NAME ______________________________

1. Mrs. Rothman is speechless because

____.

2. Check two words that tell how Perry probably felt.
   ______ disappointed
   ______ proud
   ______ eager
   ______ frightened

3. Perry says he wants to quit soccer because

____.

4. Have you ever tried to do something that was hard, or that you had to work at? What was it?

____

____

Did you get discouraged? Did you quit?

____

____

5. Do you think Perry's decision is reasonable, or do you think he is giving up too easily? Explain.

____

____

6. Mrs. Rothman probably feels
   ______ surprised ______ angry ______ entertained

7. What problem does Mrs. Rothman think Perry is having?

____

8. How does she plan to help Perry?

____

____

9. What do you think would be a good example of a power snack? Explain your choice.

____

____

Power Snack

Have you ever had a power snack?

Energy Bars

1 c. brown sugar

1 c. vegetable oil

2 eggs

2 c. oats

$1\frac{1}{2}$ c. flour

1 c. raisins

1 c. peanuts (optional)

1 c. coconut (optional)

$1\frac{1}{2}$ tsp. ground cinnamon

$1\frac{1}{2}$ tsp. ground cloves

1 tsp. baking soda

$\frac{1}{4}$ tsp. salt

Heat oven to 350° F. Grease 11" x 17" pan. Mix brown sugar, oil, and eggs until smooth. Stir in remaining ingredients. Spread mixture into pan, pressing with fingers until even. Bake until center is set, but not firm, 16–22 minutes. Remove from oven and cool for 15 minutes. Drizzle honey glaze* over bars. Let cool completely. Cut into squares. Store covered for two weeks. Or, wrap tightly and freeze for up to six months.

*Directions for honey glaze: Place $\frac{1}{4}$ c. honey and 2 T. butter or margarine in a sauce pan. Heat and stir until well blended and heated through. Drizzle over bars.

(Note: Always ask a grown-up for help in the kitchen.)

NAME ______________________

Write these steps in the correct order. (Not all of the recipe's steps are here.)

- spread mixture into pan
- drizzle glaze
- grease the pan
- mix sugar, oil, and eggs
- remove from oven and cool

1. ______________________
2. ______________________
3. ______________________
4. ______________________
5. ______________________
6. How long do the directions say to bake the bars?

____

7. The directions say to "drizzle honey glaze over bars." How did you know what honey glaze was?

____

Recipes often use short forms of words called **abbreviations**. Match the common recipe words in the box with their abbreviations.

cup	**teaspoon**
Fahrenheit	**tablespoon**

8. T. ______________________
9. c. ______________________
10. F ______________________
11. tsp. ______________________
12. The directions say, "Bake until center is set but not firm." What does this mean?

____

13. How long do the energy bars need to cool?

____

14. What is the longest you could keep these bars? What would you need to do to them?

____

____

And It's Out of the Park!

What happens at the soccer game?

1 "Okay, everybody listen up!" Coach said. It took only a moment for the team to gather. It was the first game of the season. Perry could tell that everyone was nervous and excited, just like he was.

2 "This is where all those drills pay off. You guys have dribbled to the moon and back since we started practice. You've done a good job. Now, let's remember everything we learned and play a good game. Okay?"

3 "Okay!" the team yelled, and Coach smiled. He liked their spirit.

4 "All right! Let's go, Bobcats!" Perry and his teammates roared onto the field and took their positions.

5 It seemed as if Coach's hopes were coming true. The midfielders stayed in position. The center backs defended the goal well. Coach even heard some of the other team's parents admiring how his team handled the ball.

6 Neither team scored in the first half. During the second half, there was a great play that almost put a goal on the scoreboard in the final seconds.

7 There was a terrific jumble around the ball. Perry and another player were down, leaving two other players battling it out. Perry rolled out of the way and scrambled to his feet. Just then, the ball somehow broke free and came his way. Without hesitating for a moment, he reeled back and kicked.

8 *Now that was a solid kick,* Perry thought to himself. Time seemed to stop as everyone on the field watched the arc of the ball's flight. It was beautiful. When the ball disappeared from sight, someone in the crowd yelled, "It's a home run!" The crowd and the players exploded in laughter. In the midst of all the end-of-game confusion, Perry's only thought was, *Wow, those power snacks really work.*

NAME ______________________________

1. When you read the story's title, did you guess about how the story ended? Was your guess close to being correct? Explain.

____

____

____

2. Circle the word that best describes the coach's words before the game.

   angry   encouraging

3. Have you ever been in a sporting event or a performance that didn't turn out the way you expected? Did something funny or weird happen? Write about it.

____

____

____

4. At the end of paragraph 2, Coach says that the players have "dribbled to the moon and back." This is a figure of speech. What does it mean?

____

____

5. Give one example of dialogue in the story.

____

____

   Now, give one example of a character's thought that is not spoken out loud.

____

____

6. How are the two examples in question 5 written differently from each other?

____

____

7. Why is it funny that someone in the crowd says, "It's a home run!"?

____

____

History of Soccer

Read to see how soccer had its start.

Earliest Record

1 The earliest written evidence of a soccer-like game comes from China. During the second and third centuries B.C., Chinese soldiers took part in an activity that involved kicking a ball into a small net. Historians think the game was a skill-building exercise for the soldiers.

Years of Development

2 In ancient Greece and Rome, teams of up to 27 players played a soccer-type game. In Britain hundreds of years later, during the thirteenth century A.D., whole villages played against each other. With hundreds of people playing, these games were both long and rough. Kicking, punching, and biting were common and allowed.

3 In 1331, English King Edward III passed a law in an attempt to put a stop to the popular but violent game. The king of Scotland spoke against the game a hundred years later. Queen Elizabeth I, during the late 1500s, passed a law that called for a week of jail for anyone caught playing "football," or soccer, as we call it. But the game could not be stopped.

The Modern Game Emerges

4 Two hundred and fifty years later, people in Britain were still playing a game we would recognize as soccer. A well-known English college, Eton, developed a set of rules in 1815. A number of other colleges soon agreed to use the same rules, and those schools played against each other. Finally, 50 years later, a formal association formed to oversee the playing of the game and its rules. In 1869, a rule against handling the ball with the hands transformed the game into the sport of soccer that is wildly popular all around the world.

NAME ______________________________

1. This article is mostly about
   ______ how soccer was named.
   ______ the rules of soccer.
   ______ soccer's history.

2. Historians think that soccer might have started out as a

   ____.

3. Why did King Edward III pass a law against soccer?

   ____

   ____

4. What punishment did Queen Elizabeth have for soccer players?

   ____

5. What important rule change made the game into what we know as soccer? When did it happen?

   ____

   ____

6. If you wanted to find out about the beginnings of soccer, under which heading should you look?

   ____

7. Under which heading would you find information about soccer during the last century or so?

   ____

8. Write **T** for **true** or **F** for **false** next to each statement below.
   ______ Today, you are allowed to touch the ball with your hands in soccer.
   ______ Kicking and biting were common in soccer games long ago.
   ______ In Britain, soccer is called "football."

9. At the end of paragraph 3, it says, "the game could not be stopped." Why do you think this was true?

   ____

   ____

10. What was the author's purpose for writing this article?

   ____

Why Soccer?

Why do you think soccer is so popular?

1 On what topic do more than 13 million American kids agree? Soccer! The Soccer Industry Council of America reported in 1999 that all those kids were playing organized soccer. Add adults into the mix, and you come up with more than 18 million Americans playing soccer. What makes soccer so popular?

2 First, I think there's the international appeal. Americans see that people in many other countries in the world are wildly excited about soccer. The excitement must be catching.

3 Second, soccer takes less equipment than some other sports, especially football. For that reason, it's not very costly for a kid to join a soccer team.

4 Third, parents view soccer as a safer sport than some other sports. Though accidents may occur, body contact isn't supposed to be part of the game. Therefore, fewer injuries occur.

5 Fourth, soccer appeals to both boys and girls. Though soccer was at first only a male sport (just like all other sports), soccer has caught on with girls. This is good for the sport, I think. Interest in the sport extends to whole families, so there are more players, more fans, more coaches, and so on.

6 Finally, I think there is the running factor. Running up and down a field chasing a ball is such a healthy, all-American thing to do. Kids love it, and few parents can object to it.

NAME ______________________________

1. The person who wrote this article is the **author**. The author probably wrote this article to
   ______ make you laugh.
   ______ give information.
   ______ persuade you to do something.

The author states some facts in the article. She also gives her opinion. Write **F** next to each sentence that is a fact. Write **O** next to each sentence that gives an opinion.

2. ______ Add adults into the mix, and you come up with more than 18 million Americans playing soccer.

3. ______ First, I think there's the international appeal.

4. ______ Though accidents may occur, body contact isn't supposed to be part of the game.

5. ______ And finally, I think there is the running factor.

6. Look back at the sentences you marked as opinions. What do you notice about them?

   ____

   ____

7. What is the main idea of paragraph 5?
   ______ Soccer is only for boys, just like other sports.
   ______ Soccer is a good sport for both boys and girls.
   ______ Soccer has caught on with girls.

8. Why is soccer less expensive than some other sports?

   ____

   ____

9. Look at the focus question under the title. What do you think its purpose is?

   ____

   ____

10. Have you ever played soccer? If so, tell about your experience. If not, explain why you would or would not like to try it.

   ____

   ____

A Teacher's Journal

Do you think the girls will be able to work together?

April 14

1 When my students work together on projects, everything usually works out. I had my doubts today, though, when I put Sharla, Tess, and Lee together to make a volcano. At one point, I knew something was going to blow up, and it wasn't the volcano!

2 I knew the girls weren't good friends, but I encourage my students to learn to work with all of their classmates. I could tell they felt a little shy when they sat down for their first planning meeting. Students in other groups had questions, so I didn't notice the girls for quite a few minutes. When I looked back in their direction, one looked mad, one looked sad, and one was nearly in tears. Good grief!

3 As I approached, they all started talking at once. Tess didn't want to have to touch "that icky paste" to build the volcano. Sharla had some design ideas that she couldn't get across to the other two. Lee thought they should just stop talking and get to work.

4 I calmed the girls down and suggested that they make a list of things on which they agreed. They agreed they were making a volcano out of flour, salt, and water, and that's all. They couldn't agree on the size, on a base for the volcano, or on who should get to mix the paste. Each girl had her own ideas and would not budge for the sake of working together or moving ahead.

5 By this time, the work session was over and it was time for lunch. The girls had made very little progress, and I was wondering if I had made a big mistake. Maybe this was one group of students who just couldn't work together.

NAME ______________________________

1. Do you think Sharla, Tess, and Lee will be able to work together? Write why or why not.

____

____

2. Think of times when you worked with classmates on projects. Was it hard or easy? Explain.

____

____

____

3. Would you say that you are more like Sharla—full of ideas—or more like Lee—eager to stop talking and get to work? Write why.

____

____

4. Does the teacher who is writing the journal seem thoughtful or worn out? Write why you think so.

____

____

5. At the end of the first paragraph, the teacher says, "I knew something was going to blow up, and it wasn't the volcano." What does she mean?

____

____

6. From whose point of view is this selection told?

_____ Sharla _____ Lee _____ the teacher

7. What do you predict will happen next in the story?

____

____

8. If you wrote a journal entry, what would you write about?

____

____

A Student's Journal

Read to see how the girls are moving ahead with their volcano.

April 16

1 Tess and Lee and I have to make a volcano together. Mrs. Holt put us in a group on Tuesday, and we had such a big argument! Tess was fussing about the paste, and Lee didn't want to plan anything. She just wanted to jump in and start working. It was awful. We didn't get anything done. Yesterday, Mrs. Holt made us stay in during recess so we could finish planning our volcano. Missing recess was so unfair!

2 Anyway, we finally said we would make the volcano about a foot high, and we'd add a little village around the base. That way, Tess can make the little village since she refuses to touch the volcano paste. (I think Mrs. Holt should make her.)

3 Today, Lee and I mixed up the paste. It was really goopy but kind of fun. We set up a plastic water bottle and some wadded-up aluminum foil as a base for the volcano. Then, we started plopping paste on. Tess just watched (no fair).

4 I was making my side all nice and smooth. I told Lee she should smooth out her side, too. She said, "No, Sharla, it should look lumpy, like a real mountain," just as if she were the boss. I said it would just look messy and that we should make it smooth. Well, the whole thing went downhill from there. Our paste started to dry out, and we didn't have time to finish. I suppose that means we'll have to miss recess again tomorrow, and it's all Lee's fault.

NAME ______________________

This story is written in the form of a journal entry. The person who is writing uses *I* to refer to herself. She is the **narrator**, or the person telling the story.

1. Find a sentence that tells you that the narrator actually took part in the action of the story. Write the sentence here.

   ____

   ____

2. The narrator, Sharla, disagreed with Lee about

   ____.

3. Sharla was upset because

   ____

   ____

4. Did you expect this journal to be written by Mrs. Holt, the teacher? Why or why not?

   ____

   ____

5. Why did the girls decide to make a village around the base?

   ____

6. Which of these words best describes Sharla's attitude toward the other two girls?

   ______ impatient ______ understanding ______ comforting

7. Explain how the picture adds to your understanding of the story.

   ____

   ____

8. Write **C** next to the sentence below that is the cause. Write **E** next to the sentence that is the effect.

   ______ The girls didn't make much progress on their volcano.

   ______ Mrs. Holt made the girls stay in at recess.

The Great Volcano Debate

What is the great volcano debate all about?

1 "Sharla? Lee? Tess? Can you come here for a minute, please?" Mrs. Holt called the girls to her desk. It was Friday morning.

2 "Now, you know today is the last work session on our projects, right?" she asked.

3 The girls all nodded.

4 "Are you ready to finish up?"

5 No one answered.

6 "Is there a problem?" Mrs. Holt asked, knowing perfectly well that there was a problem. She wanted the girls to put it in their own words, though.

7 Sharla glanced at the other two, and then began. "Well, I think the volcano should be smooth so it looks nice."

8 "And," jumped in Lee, "I think it should look rough and rocky, like a real mountain."

9 "I see," said Mrs. Holt, stalling for time. "What do you think, Tess?"

10 "Well, I've been making buildings for the village," she said quickly, to make sure Mrs. Holt knew she had been helping. "I think it would be neat if we could show lava flowing down toward the village, sort of like Pompeii...."

11 "Hey!" cut in Sharla, "that's a great idea. The flowing lava would be smooth. Right, Mrs. Holt?"

12 "Yes, I guess so." Mrs. Holt had never actually seen flowing lava, but it seemed reasonable.

13 Sharla continued. "The other side of the mountain, where there's no lava, would look rocky and bumpy. Right?"

14 Tess caught on. "So one side can be smooth, and the other side can be rough. Come on, you guys, let's go finish!"

15 Mrs. Holt wasn't sure, but she thought the girls might have solved their own problem.

NAME ____________________

1. In most stories, the characters have a problem. What problem do the characters in this story have?

____

2. What caused Mrs. Holt to call the girls up to her desk?

____

3. What is Tess's idea?
   ______ to show flowing lava
   ______ to make both sides smooth
   ______ to make the village larger

4. What is the result of Tess's idea?

____

____

5. Where in the story do we learn that the teacher, Mrs. Holt, knows the girls are not getting along?

____

____

6. What is the main difference in the way this story is written, compared to the other two about the same characters?
   ______ This story is told from Lee's point of view.
   ______ Sharla is not a character in this story.
   ______ It is not written as a journal entry.

7. How do you think Mrs. Holt feels about the girls solving their own problem? Explain.

____

____

8. What is the setting for this story?

____

9. The girls learned how to build a volcano by doing this project. What else do you think they learned?

____

____

The End of a Volcano Tale

What did the girls learn from their project?

1 Sharla, Tess, and Lee stood proudly behind their model volcano. Tess straightened a tiny building in the village at the base of the mountain.

2 Mrs. Holt quieted the class. "Girls, you may begin."

3 Lee felt something wiggly in her stomach. She was supposed to go first.

4 "This is our volcano," she said. *Oh, that was stupid,* thought Lee, trying not to roll her eyes. *They can probably figure that out.* "We made it this shape because that's how a lot of volcanoes are shaped."

5 Next, Sharla told about what happens when a volcano erupts. After that, Tess told about a famous volcano and the town nearby that got covered up with ash and mud.

6 When it looked as if they were done, Mrs. Holt had a question. "Can you tell about the steps you went through to complete your project, girls?"

7 The girls looked at each other. They hadn't expected this. Sharla felt her face turn red, but she spoke up.

8 "Well, at first we didn't agree about what we wanted and how we wanted to do it." Sharla shrugged. "It took us a while to make a plan and get it done."

9 Tess went on. "We figured out that everybody had a job to do."

10 "And everybody has good ideas, even if they're not what you expect," added Lee.

11 Mrs. Holt looked pleased. *It only took one volcano and two explosions to figure out how to work together,* she thought. *Not bad.*

NAME ______________________________

1. This story is mostly about
   ______ becoming best friends after working together.
   ______ what the girls learned from their project.
   ______ how a teacher helped the girls get along.

2. How do the girls feel about their volcano project?

   ____

   ____

3. When it is Lee's turn to speak, she feels
   ______ nervous.
   ______ happy.
   ______ cross.

4. Why did Sharla's face turn red when Mrs. Holt asked about how they completed their project?

   ____

   ____

5. What experiences have you had working with other people? Were there times when you didn't agree or get along? Write about it.

   ____

   ____

   ____

6. When it is Tess's turn to speak, what does she tell about?

   ____

   ____

7. Make a check mark next to the thing that happened first.
   ______ Mrs. Holt had a question.
   ______ Lee said, "This is our volcano."
   ______ Mrs. Holt looked pleased.

8. If the girls had to work together again, how do you think they would do? Explain.

   ____

   ____

Volcanoes

Read to find out why volcanoes erupt.

1 The surface of Earth is not a solid place. There are many holes, some of which allow magma to reach Earth's surface from deep inside.

2 Magma comes from deep inside Earth where it's hot. It's so hot that rocks melt. Magma is **molten**, or melted, rock. Because of the heat, there is also pressure. When things such as air, gases, or molten rock get hot, they **expand**, or get bigger. That means they need space. Weak parts of Earth's crust get pushed aside, or opened up. The magma follows the easiest path, usually along **fissures**, or cracks, toward the surface.

3 When it does reach the surface, magma is called *lava*. If there is a great deal of pressure behind the magma, it explodes through the crust's surface, sending dust, ash, lava, and rocks high into the air. When there is only a little pressure, the magma may simply bubble up and form a lava flow that spreads across the land.

4 A volcano may be **active**, or experience eruptions, on a fairly regular basis. Or it may lie **dormant**, or inactive, for hundreds of years. Scientists, called *volcanologists*, are always ready to learn more because each volcano is unique and may teach them something new about the inner workings of Earth.

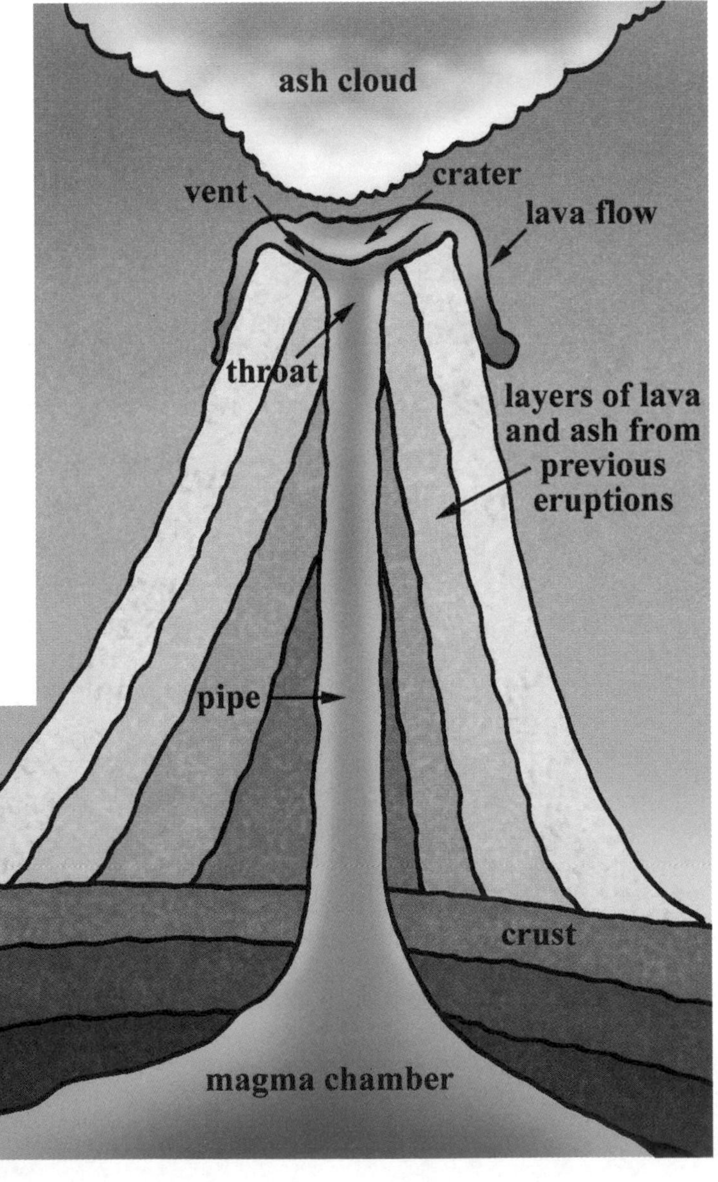

NAME ______________________________

In nonfiction writing, the author sometimes calls attention to words that the reader may not know. Those words appear in **bold** type. The author usually gives the meaning of the bold word in the same sentence.

Below are the bold words from the article. Write the meaning of each word.

1. molten ______________________________
2. expand ______________________________
3. fissures ______________________________
4. active ______________________________
5. dormant ______________________________

Write **F** next to each sentence that is a fact. Write **O** next to each sentence that is an opinion.

6. ______ Volcanic eruptions are one of the most striking natural events.
7. ______ A volcanic eruption is more frightening than a hurricane.
8. ______ Volcanoes are located in many places in the world.
9. What does the illustration show?

   ____

   ____

10. Trace with your finger the path that magma would take from under Earth's crust to the surface. Describe the path in your own words.

    ____

    ____

11. Write **C** next to the sentence below that is the cause. Write **E** next to the sentence that is the effect.

    ______ Parts of Earth's crust open up.

    ______ The molten rock gets very hot and expands.

12. What are scientists who study volcanoes called?

    ____

And the Next Unit Is...

What will Miss Eller's class learn about next?

1 The classroom hummed with the usual Monday morning activity. Students emptied their backpacks, signed in, did their morning math problems, and chattered about the weekend.

2 Miss Eller called the students to Morning Meeting and watched while they got settled. Finally, she said, "Happy Monday morning, everyone." A chorus of greetings came back.

3 "Today is a decision-making day," Miss Eller announced. A few eyebrows went up. "Today, we're ready to start a new unit." Miss Eller made sure everyone was really tuned in. "Our new unit is the natural world," said Miss Eller, and she wrote the words on the board. A hand went up.

4 "Where does the deciding come in?" Zach asked.

5 "Ah, I'm glad you asked," smiled Miss Eller. She circled her arms wide. "The natural world includes everything around us, and everything around other people, all over the world. That's too much for us to learn about, so we need to narrow our topic down quite a bit."

6 Kayla raised her hand. "Does that mean we have to pick one place in the world to learn about? I pick Alaska."

7 "That's the idea, Kayla, but even Alaska is a very big topic," answered Miss Eller. "We would have to narrow that down even further. Yes, Zach?"

8 "Would a grasshopper's knees be narrow enough?" Everyone giggled.

9 "Well, that might be a little too narrow, but grasshoppers would be an excellent topic. I want all of you to think about one thing in the natural world that you want to learn about. We'll talk about this again after lunch. Okay?" Everyone nodded.

10 "Now, whose turn is it to do the weather chart?" As Miss Eller started the daily routine, twenty-two busy brains were thinking up ideas.

NAME ___________________________

Write the best word to complete each sentence below.

1. The students were especially ______________ on Monday morning. (noisy, quiet, confused)
2. Miss Eller wrote the topic on the ______________. (notebook, list, board)
3. The teacher waved her ______________ all around. (ruler, book, arms)
4. Zach was only ______________ about the grasshopper's knees. (wondering, kidding, thinking)
5. What do Miss Eller's students do as they begin their day? Find five details from the story and list them in order.

____

____

____

6. What do you think will happen after lunch, when the students meet to talk about their new unit?

____

____

7. What kind of decision do the students need to make?

____

8. Why does Miss Eller tell Kayla that Alaska might not be the best topic?

____

9. According to Miss Eller, what does the natural world include?

____

____

10. Is this story realistic? Why or why not?

____

____

So Many Ideas

Read to find out what everyone wants to study.

1 Miss Eller's students clattered in from lunch recess. Balls and jump ropes landed in the recess basket. A line formed at the water fountain as hot and thirsty children waited for their turn to cool down. Miss Eller's quiet presence at the meeting rug was a signal for everyone to settle down and join her.

2 Miss Eller began when all mouths stopped, and all eyes were on her. "Have all of you been thinking about the natural world and what you would like to learn about?" Heads nodded and some hands shot up. "Tara?"

3 "I want to study wild animals," Tara stated simply.

4 Miss Eller challenged her. "There are many, many wild animals. Did you have any particular ones in mind?"

5 Tara looked at the ceiling and thought for a moment. "Just the cute, fuzzy ones that live in the woods."

6 "Hmm, well, that narrows it down. Enzo?"

7 Enzo was sure of himself. "Snakes. Just the coolest ones."

8 "Okay," nodded Miss Eller. "Snakes are certainly part of the natural world, and you narrowed down the topic a bit already. Anyone else? Andy?"

9 "Trees are an important part of the natural world, right?" asked Andy.

10 "Yes," agreed Miss Eller.

11 "But there are too many kinds," continued Andy, "so I would narrow them down to redwood trees. They're special because they're so big."

12 "They certainly are," said Miss Eller. "Anyone else?"

13 Hand after hand went up. Everyone had a different idea. Miss Eller listened carefully and thought to herself, *How will we ever agree on what to study?*

NAME ______________________

1. Which of the students' ideas do you like best? Write why.

____

____

2. Write **R** next to the sentences that tell about what Miss Eller's students could do for their study of the natural world. Write **M** next to the sentences that are about made-up things.

   ______ Isaac goes to the South Pole.

   ______ Tasha collects seeds.

   ______ Justin sets up a bird feeder.

   ______ Megan climbs the Alps.

3. What does this sentence from the story tell you about Miss Eller?
   "Miss Eller's quiet presence at the meeting rug was a signal for everyone to settle down and join her."

____

____

4. Look for another sentence that tells you something about Miss Eller. What does it tell you?

____

____

5. Why does Andy narrow down his topic?

____

6. What is this story mostly about?

   ______ the natural world

   ______ how Miss Eller gets her class to behave

   ______ a class coming up with ideas for a new unit of study

7. What problem does Miss Eller have at the end of the story?

____

8. If you were the teacher, how would you solve the problem?

____

____

____

Too Many Ideas!

How will the class ever decide what to study?

1 Miss Eller stared at the board. It looked like a maze. She didn't know where to begin.

2 "That's quite a pack of ideas," said a voice from over her shoulder. It was Mrs. Samm, the fourth-grade teacher.

3 "Oh, hello, Gina," smiled Miss Eller. "I want the students to help decide what to study, but now I have to narrow this down to something we can manage." Miss Eller shook her head.

4 "It's too bad they can't all follow their own ideas," Mrs. Samm said. "The students will be more eager to learn if they're working on topics that they're already interested in." Mrs. Samm turned to go. "Well, good luck. I hope you can sell your solution, whatever it is."

5 Miss Eller was so distracted she didn't even notice Mrs. Samm leave. *Sell my solution....that's it!* Miss Eller snapped her fingers and finished getting ready for the day.

6 Later, at Morning Meeting, Miss Eller started to sell her solution.

7 "Andy, how much do you want to study redwoods?" she asked.

8 Andy shrugged. "A lot, I guess."

9 Miss Eller turned to Tara. "What about you and your fuzzy animals?"

10 "Oh, they're so cute," said Tara, wrinkling up her nose. "They're my favorite things."

11 "Okay," said Miss Eller to the whole group, "you're going to have to convince us that your topic is the best one. Each of you is going to do some research on your own topic this week. Then, you'll give a "sales pitch" to the class and try to convince us to choose your topic to study." She scanned the faces all around her. *Are they buying it?* she wondered.

12 "Miss Eller?" asked Enzo. "Can I give out plastic snakes to help convince people?"

13 *Sold.*

NAME ______________________________

1. This story is mostly about
   ______ solving a problem.
   ______ how to do research.
   ______ getting ready for school.

2. Why does Miss Eller let the students offer so many ideas?

____

____

____

3. Write in your own words what Miss Eller's solution is.

____

____

____

4. What are the students supposed to do during their sales pitch?

____

____

____

5. Based on the story, do you think Miss Eller is a good teacher? Back up your answer with events from the story.

____

____

____

6. Andy wants to study ______________________________.

7. Tara wants to study ______________________________.

8. What does Enzo ask at the end of the story? Why does this make Miss Eller think that her idea was a success?

____

____

____

Forest Mammals

Do you know what a mammal is?

Common Characteristics

1 What does a moose have in common with a porcupine? How about a bear with a mouse? How can more than 4,000 different kinds of mammals have much of anything in common? In fact, mammals have four distinct characteristics:

1. Mammals have warm blood, which means they can maintain a steady body temperature.
2. Mammals have backbones.
3. Female mammals produce milk to feed their babies.
4. Mammals have fur or hair, though the amount of it varies widely.

North American Forest Dwellers

2 Forest mammals are alike in that they live in the same natural conditions, or **habitat**. Trees and the leafy undergrowth provide shelter and food for the many types of mammals that live in a North American forest.

3 **Insect eaters** Moles and shrews are just two types of **insectivores** that live on or under the forest floor. They find insects in the dirt or in rotting tree trunks or leaf matter.

4 **Gnawing animals** This large family of mammals, called **rodents**, includes beavers, squirrels, mice, and porcupines. Whether on the ground or in trees, these animals gnaw on nuts, seeds, and branches with their strong front teeth.

5 **Hare-like animals** Rabbits and hares make up this group. Leafy sprouts and sometimes the bark of young trees are the main diet of these animals.

6 **Meat eaters** In North America, the largest meat eaters, or **carnivores**, are bears and mountain lions. Wolves and coyotes are also members of this group. They eat smaller mammals such as rabbits, mice, and moles.

7 **Hoofed animals** In North America, moose and deer are the most common forest-dwelling hoofed animals. The forest provides both shelter and food for them.

NAME ______________________

1. What four common characteristics do mammals have?

____

____

In the article, the author showed some words in bold type. The meanings of those words are given as well. Find the meanings of the words, and write them here.

2. habitat ______________________________________

____

3. insectivores __________________________________

____

4. rodents ______________________________________

____

5. carnivores ____________________________________

____

6. Hoofed animals are named for the kind of ______________ they have.

7. Give one example of each kind of forest dweller.

insect eaters: ______________ gnawing animals: ______________

hare-like animals: ______________ meat eaters: ______________

hoofed animals: ______________

8. Why do you think a forest is a good habitat for many different kinds of mammals?

____

____

9. Think about what you know about mammals. Name two kinds of mammals that are not mentioned in the article.

______________________ and ______________________

10. **Meat eaters eat smaller mammals, such as rabbits, mice, and moles.** Is this sentence a fact or an opinion?

____

Snakes: Love Them or Leave Them?

Why do you think snakes are not popular?

1 I think it is safe to say that most people really don't like snakes. It would be hard to find a person who is neutral, or simply doesn't care one way or the other. What I can't figure out is why something that doesn't even have any legs causes such alarm.

2 Snakes are reptiles, of course, not mammals. Do you think there is some ancient hatred between mammals and reptiles? Maybe their cold-bloodedness is what makes us dislike snakes. Or perhaps age-old stories about frightening creatures with scales cause us to turn away from our neighbors, the snakes.

3 Snakes are quite useful, but that doesn't seem to matter. Snakes help control the rodent population. Without snakes, perhaps we would be overrun with mice. Most of us, however, would rather see a mouse than a snake.

4 The poison argument is a strong one. Some snakes are poisonous, and people all over the world do die from snake bites each year. However, the poisonous varieties are only a small percentage of the world's snakes. We can't say the whole batch is bad just because of a few rotten ones.

5 And what do we do with the people who really like snakes? They like snakes even more strongly than we dislike them. These people learn about them, seek them out, and observe them. Why? The only reason I can think of is that these people are truly generous and open-minded. They are able to put aside differences and welcome the snake as a fellow living being.

6 Whatever the reason for our like or dislike, snakes are a vital part of the circle of life. They would prefer to be left alone, and that is what we should do. If you're lucky, you might not run across more than a few of them in an entire lifetime. That would be fine with most of us.

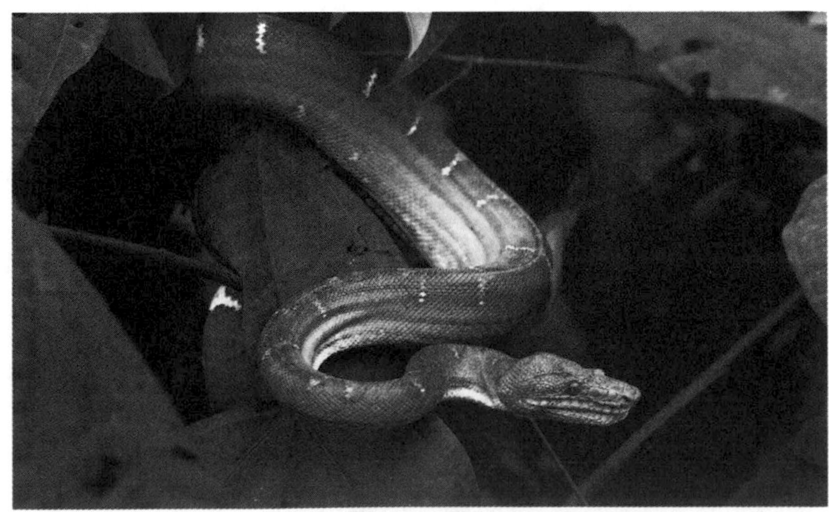

NAME ______________________

The author of this article chose to share her own point of view. Find a sentence in which the author uses the word *I*. What idea is the author sharing in that sentence?

1. The sentence begins with

   ____.

   The author is saying ______________________________

   ____.

2. Do you think the author likes snakes, dislikes snakes, or is neutral? Write a sentence from the article that supports your answer.

   ____

   ____

Write **F** next to each sentence that is a fact. Write **O** next to each sentence that is an opinion.

3. ______ People dislike snakes because they have no legs.
4. ______ Snakes control the rodent population.
5. ______ Not meeting many snakes is a good thing.
6. Name one difference between mammals and reptiles.

   ____

   ____

7. What is one way in which snakes are useful?

   ____

8. What is the main idea of paragraph 4?

   ______ If you get bitten by a poisonous snake, seek medical help.

   ______ Some snakes are poisonous, but that's not a good reason to dislike all snakes.

   ______ Poisonous snakes are very vicious.

9. Tell how you feel about snakes and why.

   ____

   ____

   ____

Redwood Giants

Read to learn about America's biggest trees.

1 From a seed that is smaller than a pea grows the tallest of trees. The coast redwood is the unchallenged giant of North America's trees.

What's special about redwoods?

2 Redwoods are special for a couple of reasons. The first is their size. Imagine standing next to a tree that is the height of a 20- or 30-story building. The second is their age. Redwoods commonly make it to 600 years or so. Some have been found that are more than 2,000 years old.

Where do redwoods grow?

3 To find a coast redwood, you'll have to go to Oregon or California. A strip of coastline about 450 miles long and up to 35 miles wide is home to the redwoods. Coast redwoods do not grow anywhere else in the world.

Why do redwoods grow there?

4 The coast of the Pacific Ocean provides a special environment for the redwoods. Cool, moist air comes off the ocean and keeps the trees moist all year. That is important because almost all of the area's rain falls between October and May. During the dry summer months, the trees depend on moisture from the thick fog that often hangs over the coast.

How do redwoods survive?

5 Redwoods have a couple of built-in protection systems. Most of a redwood's branches and leaves are high up on the tree. This keeps them safe from forest fires. Also, the bark of a mature redwood tree is as much as 12 inches thick. The thick covering protects the lower part of the tree from fire damage. Redwoods are safe from insect damage because the wood contains a bitter-tasting chemical called *tannin*.

What should I do?

6 If you ever get a chance, visit a redwood forest. Look among the tree trunks and imagine who might have camped there a thousand years ago. Look upward and just imagine how high the trees might grow if we preserve and protect them.

NAME ______________________________

1. To see a redwood tree, you have to go to ______________________________.

2. Why do redwoods grow there?

____

____

3. What might happen if someone tried to grow a redwood tree in Kansas or Missouri, for example?

____

____

4. What do you think is most special about redwood trees? Write why.

____

____

5. Why do you think the author chose to use questions for the headings?

____

____

6. If you want to find out what conditions redwoods need to grow, under which heading would you look?

____

7. If you wonder what the big deal is about redwoods, under which heading should you look?

____

8. What three objects are shown in the diagram?

____

9. What is the author's purpose for writing this selection?

_____ to entertain

_____ persuade

_____ to inform

10. About how long can a redwood live?

____

Problem Solved

What will Miss Eller decide the class should study?

1 So far, Miss Eller's idea had worked out. Her students had done some research on whatever they wanted to know about the natural world. They had all really enjoyed uncovering facts about snails or redwood trees or grasshoppers. And Enzo's plastic snakes had been a big hit.

2 Now, it all fell back to Miss Eller, though. She had to decide whose ideas to accept and whose to reject. She thought back on the students' reports and tried to sort them into groups. Furry things in this group, and crawling things in that group? No, that didn't really work.

3 Suddenly, her gaze shifted and she realized that the answer was right in front of her. A poster on the wall showed a lush woodland scene that included many different kinds of trees, forest creatures, birds, and, yes, even some snakes and crawly things. Miss Eller smiled. *A picture is worth a thousand words—or a thousand ideas,* she thought. She had the solution.

4 After lunch, the students gathered on the meeting rug. "What if I told you that we are going to have one topic, but that you are all going to be able to study what you want?"

5 "How can that be?" questioned Tara. "We all had different ideas."

6 Miss Eller shrugged. "It all depends on how you group things together. What if our topic is 'Redwood Forests'? What do you suppose lives in a redwood forest?"

7 Hands shot up left and right. Everything the students could think of fit into Miss Eller's topic: redwood trees, of course, cute and fuzzy mammals, snails, snakes—you name it.

8 Within a few weeks, the classroom had been transformed. A sign appeared outside the classroom door.

Welcome to our
redwood forest.
If something lives, grows, eats, breathes, or crawls in a redwood forest, we know all about it.
Come on in.

NAME ______________________________

Complete each sentence with the correct word.

author	**dialogue**	**narrator**

1. When characters speak, their words make up the story's

   ______________________.

2. The person who wrote the story is the ______________________.

3. Within the story, the person or character who tells the story is the

   ______________________.

4. In most stories, the main character has a problem. Miss Eller's problem is that

   ____

5. Look at the illustration. What did Miss Eller's students do during their study of redwood forests?

   ____

   ____

   ____

6. Where did Miss Eller get the idea of how to solve the problem?

   ____

7. How do you think Miss Eller's class feels about the project?

   ______ excited

   ______ worried

   ______ upset

8. The last paragraph says that the classroom had been transformed. What does this mean?

   ____

9. Write **C** next to the sentence below that is the cause. Write **E** next to the sentence that is the effect.

   ______ Students raise their hands to answer the question.

   ______ Miss Eller asks what lives in a redwood forest.

The Hamster from Room 144

What is unusual about this hamster?

1 I always knew Felix was special. He had been Mrs. Raymond's class pet for about 24 years. This summer, I was the lucky one who got to take him home. Felix, by the way, is a hamster.

2 As I said, I always knew he was special. Every school day when I checked on him, he would say, "Good morning, Tommy." That struck me as a little odd. When I saw him sitting in his cage counting on his claws during math class, I knew something was up for sure.

3 On the first day of summer, I took my allowance and my mom to the pet store. I bought some tunnels to add to Felix's cage. Felix loved his tunnels. By the end of the first week, Mom said, "Enough already," so I stopped adding tunnels. There were 376 feet of them.

4 One night, I couldn't fall asleep, so I went down to talk to Felix. He was running on his wheel. He apologized for not being able to chat, but he was trying to break a speed record. I watched for a while. I clocked him at 41 miles per hour.

5 The next night, Dad came down to watch. He had a brilliant idea. He hooked up a generator to Felix's wheel. Now, Felix makes electricity for us. We haven't had a bill from the electric company for two months.

6 Here's another reason I knew Felix was special. Back in Room 144, whenever it was time for music, I would see Felix tapping his little claws against the bars of the cage. He had excellent rhythm. During the summer, Felix took to writing his own songs. He even wrote one for Mrs. Raymond.

7 Now that summer is almost over, I'm kind of sad about having to take Felix back to Mrs. Raymond. Dad says he'll miss not having to pay any electric bills. Felix says not to worry. He has a plan for a new generator. Good old Felix.

NAME ____________________

In a tall tale, the author uses details that can't possibly be true to make the story funny. This is called **exaggeration**. Exaggeration is what makes a tall tale a tall tale.

1. Caleb, the narrator, tells us that the hamster has lived for 24 years. That is an exaggeration. Find another exaggeration in the story.

____

____

2. Look at what you wrote for question 1. Why or how is it an exaggeration?

____

____

____

3. What was the author's purpose in writing this story?

____

____

4. Do you think this story is realistic or a fantasy? Explain why.

____

____

5. **Personification** means giving human characteristics to an animal or a thing. Give two examples of how the author personifies Felix.

____

____

6. In the story, how does Felix make electricity for Caleb's family?

____

____

7. **Felix is a musical hamster.** Find a line from the story to support this statement.

____

____

Caring for a Pet Hamster

What does it take to care for a hamster?

1 You and your parents agree that you are ready for a pet. A dog is too big. Mom is allergic to cats. So a hamster is everyone's number one choice. What will it take to keep your new pet safe and happy?

2 Choose a hamster from a pet store that is clean and whose staff seems to know about the animals and is willing to answer your questions. If the hamsters are not used to being handled, you probably want to choose a younger one. You'll be able to tame and handle a younger one more easily than an older one.

3 Before you get your hamster, you should have its new home all set up. Hamsters need several pieces of equipment, but the only one that is somewhat expensive is the cage. Here are the items your hamster must have: a cage, bedding (wood shavings), nesting material (cotton), an exercise wheel, a water bottle, a food dish, and food.

4 Almost all of your hamster's life will be spent in the cage, and it needs room to move around. Buy the largest cage you can afford. A wire cage is best if you have a draft-free place for it. If the cage has to sit near a vent, window, or door, then a plastic or glass type with a screen top is better.

5 Make sure that your hamster has fresh water at all times. A general hamster mix from the pet store will make up most of your pet's diet. Beyond that, learn what other foods you can give as treats. Some examples are carrots, raisins, cheese, dog biscuits, and acorns. In general, do not feed your hamster sweets or prepared foods, such as crackers or chips.

6 With daily food and water, regular attention, and a weekly cage cleaning, your hamster should be a happy addition to your household for several years.

NAME ______________________

1. What do you know about taking care of a pet? How is taking care of a hamster the same or different from taking care of other kinds of pets?

____

____

____

2. In the wild, hamsters sleep during the day and gather food during the night. Pet hamsters tend to follow the same schedule. If someone is thinking of getting a hamster, why is this important information to know?

____

____

____

The author forgot to include headings in the article. Write where each heading should go.

3. **Equipment** should go before the ______________ paragraph.

4. **Feeding Time** should go before the ______________ paragraph.

5. **Choosing a Pet** should go before the ______________ paragraph.

6. List the equipment you'll need to buy for your hamster.

____

____

____

7. The ______________ is the most expensive thing you will need to purchase.

8. What are some examples of good treats for a hamster?

____

9. After reading this article, would you like to own a hamster? Why or why not?

____

____

____

Skyway Sweeper

What does Frederick think about as he works?

1 *Swish, swush. Swish, swush.* Frederick had always thought the broom had two different sounds to it. *Swish* was the outward stroke; *swush* was the inward stroke. It was the only sound he heard all day, really. The padded plastorub floors of the skyways didn't make any noise. Most people wore shoes made of plastorub as well, so there was no chance of making a sound.

2 Noise had become a big issue about a century ago. There were so many people making so much noise that no one could stand it. People wore ear plugs. New illnesses were blamed on noise pollution. Governments passed laws against noise. Then, a team of scientists came up with plastorub. People put it everywhere, and the noise died down.

3 Between plastorub and the big building boom, things were pretty quiet now. The buildings were so big and so tall that people didn't even have to go outside. People lived, worked, and shopped all in the same building.

4 Not Frederick, though. Frederick was a sweeper. Each night he slept in a different sweeper's lodge as he made his rounds from skyway to skyway. *Swish, swush. Swish, swush.*

5 Frederick liked his job. He liked seeing how things changed from one year to the next. Buildings went up or came down. Skyways sprouted and branched off to new places. He always liked the view, no matter what it was.

6 Through all of his sweeping travels, though, Frederick had never set foot on the ground. He had seen it a few times, through a window, but he had never actually stepped on it. People said it was hard and unpleasant. He imagined taking off his plastorub shoes and walking barefoot, just to feel the solid planet underneath him. Frederick wondered what it was like to hear a footstep.

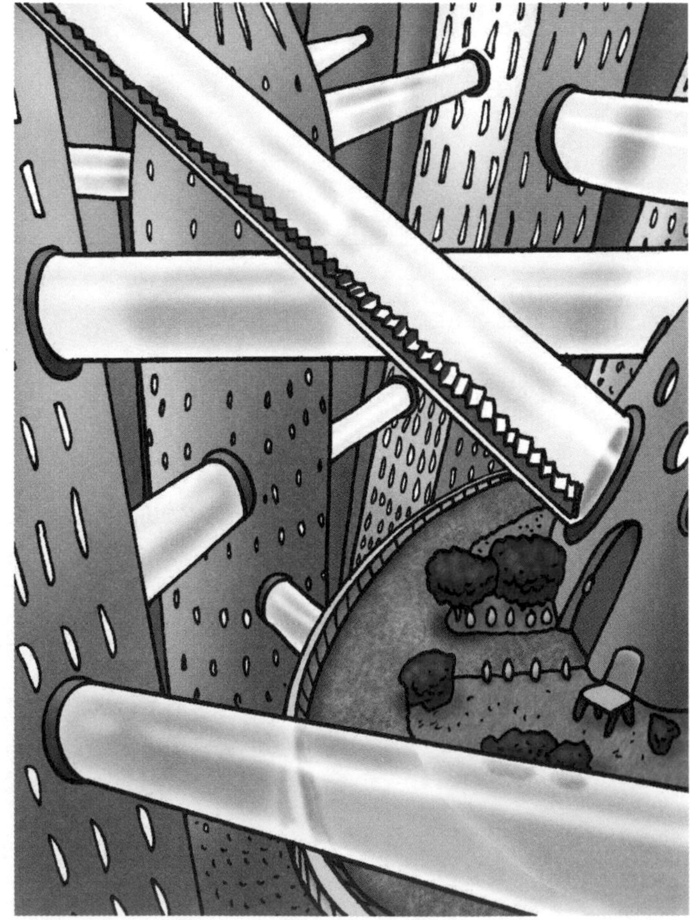

NAME ______________________

1. The story gives details about Frederick and the world in which he lives. Number these details in the order in which the story gives them.
   ______ Noise had been a problem.
   ______ Frederick liked his job.
   ______ Frederick is a skyway sweeper.
   ______ The skyway floors are padded.
   ______ People stayed inside all the time.
   ______ Frederick had never stepped on the ground.

2. As the story gives details, several sounds are mentioned. What are they?

   ____

   ____

3. Which of these best describes the story?
   ______ realistic fiction
   ______ a fairy tale
   ______ science fiction

4. Write **C** next to the sentence below that is the cause. Write **E** next to the sentence that is the effect.
   ______ Noise had become a big issue.
   ______ Plastorub was put down everywhere, and the noise died down.

5. What does Frederick like about his job?

   ____

   ____

   ____

6. What is the setting for this story?

   ____

7. Would you like to live in a world of skyways, like Frederick does? Explain.

   ____

   ____

   ____

   ____

Rooftop Keeper

Read to find out what sirt *is and how Frederick feels about it.*

1 *Sssssssssssssss.* The sirt sifted between Frederick's fingers. He was used to the feel and the sound of it, but he wondered...well, there was no use in wondering.

2 Real dirt had been used up long ago. There were so many people to feed, and there were so many buildings covering up the ground. The whole idea of farming had been reinvented. That's when sirt was invented. The scientists called it *sirt* to make people think of *soil* and *dirt,* but most people didn't know what was in it. Sirt did make things grow, though, and that's what counted.

3 When he wasn't sweeping skyways, Frederick was the Head Rooftop Keeper for Building Q4-S621-B88. It was his job to grow fresh fruits and vegetables and supply them to the families who lived down below. Frederick took pride in his crops. Nothing pleased him more than when someone commented on his shiny apples or his crunchy carrots.

4 *Sssssss* went the sirt again as Frederick scooped and sifted, preparing the surface for some new seeds. He crinkled his nose as the faint chemical smell of the sirt reached him. He had read about people who, a long time ago, would kiss the dirt and talk to it. Frederick couldn't imagine kissing sirt. He couldn't imagine...well, he couldn't imagine a lot of things.

5 What did wet dirt feel like? Sirt didn't change, whether it was wet or dry. That was the chemicals, Frederick supposed. Did dirt run through your fingers just like sirt? *Ah, there's no use wondering,* he scolded himself. Frederick shook the sirt off his hands and took hold of his broom handle to begin the day's work. *Still, I wonder...*

NAME ______________________

1. Write **R** next to the sentences that tell about something real. Write **M** next to the sentences that are about made-up things.
   ______ People do not know what dirt feels like.
   ______ The whole world is covered up with buildings.
   ______ People grow vegetables in gardens.
   ______ People stay indoors and never have to go outside.

In some stories, the problem is obvious. For example, maybe the character breaks an arm and has to learn how to write with the other hand, or something like that. In this story, the problem is not as obvious.

2. What problem does this character have?

____

____

3. According to the story, what is the word *sirt* supposed to make people think of?

____

4. In the story, how did all the real dirt get used up?

____

____

5. How could you describe Frederick?
   ______ lazy
   ______ a hard worker
   ______ hilarious

6. What effect does water have on sirt?

____

7. Reread the last paragraph. What do you predict will happen next?

____

____

8. In what time period do you think this story takes place? Why?

____

____

The Dirt on Soil

Read to find out what soil is.

1 Are dirt and soil the same thing? If you ask a gardener, she'll say that dirt is what is under her fingernails. Your mother will say that dirt is what you tracked into the house after walking through the garden. The gardener, however, will say that the stuff out in the garden is soil.

2 The dictionary says that soil is the upper layer of Earth's surface. Scientists and gardeners know it as the layer in which things grow. In most of North America, the soil is from 6 to 10 inches thick.

3 Soil is made up of three main parts. First, there are minerals. These minerals come from nearby rocks that have been broken into tiny pieces, or **fragments**, by rain, frost, sun, or wind. Mineral pieces might be large, in the form of gravel, or tiny, such as the small particles that make up clay.

4 The second part of soil is the remains of dead plants and animals. When plants and animals die, they provide food for countless living organisms. These organisms make up the third part of soil. Most of them are bacteria, but fungi, insects, and earthworms do their part as well. The job of the living organisms is to break down the dead materials. The result is **humus**, a dark, slightly sticky substance that helps plants grow in the soil.

5 So, now you have the dirt on soil. It is not just a lifeless thing lying on the ground outside. It is full of life itself and is the source of all growing things.

NAME ______________________

Nonfiction articles and books sometimes have words in bold type. The author is pointing out a new or important word. Find the two bold words in the article. Then, look nearby for their meanings. Write them here.

1. Bold word: ______________________

   Meaning: ______________________

2. Bold word: ______________________

   Meaning: ______________________

3. What three things make up the soil?

   ____

   ____

4. When was the last time you dug in the soil? What did you see there?

   ____

   ____

5. Now, look at the picture on page 72. What do you see there?

   ____

   ____

6. How does this compare with what you saw when you dug in the soil yourself?

   ____

   ____

7. How thick is the soil in most of North America?

   ______ to ______ inches

8. What organisms help break down the dead material?

   ____

   ____

9. Write **T** for **true** or **F** for **false** next to each statement below.

   ______ Not everyone has the same definition of dirt and soil.

   ______ Minerals come from rocks that have been broken into fragments.

   ______ Soil does not contain any living things.

   ______ Humus is harmful to plants.

Frederick's Secret

Read to see how Frederick's dream leads to Frederick's secret.

1 No sunlight reached the ground. Frederick hadn't stopped to think about that. Of course, it made sense, though. The buildings were so tall and so close together. But more than the lack of sunlight, it was the airlessness that Frederick noticed. It was so still and stale that Frederick almost had to work to breathe.

2 The idea had come about slowly. The *swish-swush* of his broom up in the skyways had become *sirt-dirt, sirt-dirt*. Frederick had grown up with sirt, the special chemical mix that was used in place of dirt in his rooftop garden. But to feel the ground and touch real dirt—that's what he thought about constantly, and that's what brought about his plan.

3 After many weeks of thinking and of finding courage, Frederick had made his way down to the surface. Now, he followed streets and paths, looking for a bare patch of ground. It took so long. He began to panic, thinking he would never find one. Then, two more left turns and Frederick's dream came true.

4 Frederick ran to the small bare patch of dirt, missed somehow by the builders years ago. Tears welled up in his eyes as he fell to his knees, touching the ground with his fingers, smelling it, even kissing it. Then, his shoes were off, and he was standing, bare-footed, wiggling his toes, stomping his feet, actually hearing the soft thud of his own footsteps. Frederick stood there, looking straight upward through his tears, until the sky began to darken. Then, he filled his shoes with dirt and made his way back to his rooftop garden.

5 Six months later, Frederick received an award from the government. His fruits and vegetables were judged to be outstanding in appearance, flavor, and nutritional value. The news headline read as follows:

NAME ____________________

1. Where does this story take place?

2. What is Frederick's dream?

3. What is Frederick's secret?

4. Is it easy or difficult for Frederick to find a patch of dirt?

5. Why does Frederick receive an award?

6. The story doesn't tell us what happens after Frederick fills his shoes with dirt. What details from the story help you figure it out?

7. Write two words to describe how Frederick feels when he finds real dirt.

Buildings: From Tall to Taller

Read to find out about tall buildings.

1 Looking up at them might make you dizzy. Looking down from the top of them might make you dizzy, too. Tall buildings are a wonder, whether looking up or down.

Two Ways to Get Tall

2 Today's skyscrapers trace their roots all the way back to the 1880s. During that decade, two things happened. First, a man named William Jenney had the idea of using a steel frame to hold up the walls and floors of a building. Then, he added just a thin "skin" for the outer walls—instead of heavy stone or brick—to enclose the building. Jenney's design made it possible to make larger, taller buildings.

3 The second thing that happened was that elevator design improved. This, too, made it possible to make buildings taller.

How Tall Is Tall?

4 Back in 1883, Jenney's first tall building was 10 stories high. Imagine what he would think of today's skyscrapers, topping out at 160 stories.

5 Tall buildings are measured from the sidewalk level at the front entrance. At the top, spires are measured, but antennae and flag poles do not count. In 2010, a new building took first place on the list. Burj Khalifa, at 2,716 feet tall, beats the previous first-place winner by more than a thousand feet.

NAME ______________________

1. The author's purpose was probably to
   ______ entertain.
   ______ give information.
   ______ persuade.

2. Improvements in elevator design made it possible to build taller buildings because ____

   ____

   ____.

3. What ideas did William Jenney have that changed how tall buildings could be?

   ____

   ____

   ____

4. Is this article fiction or nonfiction?

   ____

5. How tall was Jenney's first tall building?

   ____

6. Write **C** next to the sentence below that is the cause. Write **E** next to the sentence that is the effect.
   ______ Buildings could be made taller.
   ______ Elevator design improved.

7. In paragraph 5, the article says that spires are included. Look up *spire* in a dictionary. Write the definition below.

   ____

   ____

Magic with Flowers

What are Josh and Gary trying to do?

1 *"Ala-ka-ZAM!"* said Gary, trying to make his voice sound big. He waved his arms in and out in what he hoped was a fancy pattern, and then tapped the box sitting on the table with a magic wand. He held his breath. The box jiggled a little. Then, the table jiggled a little.

2 *"Ahhhhh!"* The exclamation erupted from under the table.

3 "What's the matter?" called Gary. "Did it work?"

4 Gary's friend Josh came out from under the table. His hair was wet. His shirt was wet. He was holding a vase of fake flowers. "Well, it worked if you don't count spilling water all over," Josh grumbled. The boys had put water in the vase because they thought it would make it all seem more real.

5 "Maybe we should use real flowers," suggested Gary.

6 "They'd just wilt," Josh shook his head.

7 Gary shrugged. "Yeah, I guess so. Aside from spilling, how did it go under there?"

8 Josh told what had happened. When Gary tapped the box, Josh was supposed to open the secret door on the bottom of the box and pull the vase of flowers down, and then close up the box again. But the bottom had gotten stuck and the vase had tipped. The boys sat down to rethink their plan.

9 The boys had thought the old broken table was almost too good to be true. Its worn-out wicker top had a hole that was just the right size for covering with the box as well as for making stuff disappear by pulling it through.

10 "This whole magic thing just isn't as easy as I thought it would be," noted Gary.

11 "Yeah, I know," Josh agreed. "How do you suppose the real magicians did it? They made stuff disappear all the time."

12 An idea popped into Gary's head and his face brightened. "Maybe it is the fake flowers. The real ones used real stuff, like rabbits. We need a rabbit. Go get Wiggles!"

NAME ______________________________

1. This story is mostly about
   ______ two boys trying to do a magic trick.
   ______ a boy teaching another boy a magic trick.
   ______ how to do a magic trick.

2. Josh got wet because ______________________________

   ____.

3. Why was Josh under the table?

   ____

   ____

4. Write **C** next to the sentence below that is the cause. Write **E** next to the sentence that is the effect.
   ______ The vase tipped and got Josh wet.
   ______ The bottom of the box got stuck.

5. Why were the boys so excited about the old table they found?

   ____

   ____

6. Doing magic is (easier, harder) than the boys had expected.

7. Gary thinks that he and Josh need real things, so he tells Josh to go get a real

   ____.

8. Read the sentences below. Write **F** next to sentences that are facts and **O** next to sentences that are opinions.
   ______ Gary held his breath.
   ______ The boys should use real flowers.
   ______ Being a magician is hard work.
   ______ Josh's hair was wet.

9. What do you think will happen next?

   ____

   ____

   ____

Magic with Wiggles

Read to see whether Josh and Gary's new trick works.

1 *Well, okay,* thought Josh. Every magician they had ever read about had used rabbits. Josh couldn't believe they hadn't thought of Wiggles earlier. He had a good feeling about this.

2 Gary put a lettuce leaf in the box, and then Josh put Wiggles in the box and closed one of the top flaps. Josh got into position under the table so he could pull Wiggles through the hole in the bottom of the box and make him disappear.

3 Gary cleared his throat and raised his arms slowly. *"Ala-ka-...."*

4 "Hey, wait," called Josh from underneath the table. He crawled part way out. "Maybe we should try a new word. A rabbit-y word."

5 "A rabbit-y word?" Gary looked doubtful. "Like what?"

6 "Well, I don't know." Josh thought for a moment. "How about *rabbit-o-zam*?

7 *"Rabbit-o-ZAM!"* Gary tried it out. Both boys shook their heads.

8 Josh tried again. *"Shish-rabbit-ka-zam!"* Nope.

9 *"Abra-ca-DAB-rabbit!"* tried Gary.

10 "Abra-ca-DAB-rabbit?" Josh was laughing so hard he could barely get the word out.

11 After a good laughing spell, the boys got back down to business. They agreed to go back to good old *abracadabra.*

12 Josh took his position, and Gary did his part, complete with arms waving and stick tapping. The box jiggled a tiny bit. The table jiggled.

13 *"Ahhhhh!"* The cry from under the table was truly alarming.

14 "Now what's wrong?" cried Gary.

15 *"It worked!"* screamed Josh, scrambling out from under the table. *"It worked! Wiggles is gone!"*

16 "It worked?" cried Gary, and he dived under the table in disbelief. When he came out, the boys did a little dance, and then they bowed to the imaginary crowd, quite certain that they heard wild clapping.

17 Wiggles had, indeed, disappeared.

NAME ______________________

1. How was the magic trick supposed to work?

____

2. What actually happened?

____

____

Write the best word to complete each sentence below.

3. They should have thought of Wiggles ______________. (brighter, sooner, calmer)

4. The magic words made the boys ______________ so hard. (laugh, lame, learn)

5. It made Gary feel like a real magician when he ______________ his arms. (waved, cried, tapped)

6. The boys couldn't ______________ Wiggles was gone. (agree, scramble, believe)

7. Write **R** next to the sentences that tell about something real. Write **M** next to the sentences that are about made-up things.
   ______ Rabbits eat lettuce.
   ______ Rabbits disappear and reappear.
   ______ Magicians say magic words.

8. In the story, who is the magician, and who is the assistant?

____

____

9. Do you think the boys were surprised that Wiggles was actually gone? Why or why not?

____

____

10. Which words best describe the boys?
   ______ good-natured
   ______ sneaky
   ______ irritated

11. What do you think will happen next in the story?

____

____

Houdini

What made Harry Houdini so great?

1 Do you believe in magic? The greatest magician of all time didn't. Harry Houdini was known as "The King of Cards" and "The Great Escape Artist." But he was the first to say that his magic tricks were tricks, not magic.

2 Houdini's early interest in magic tricks led him to read about famous magicians. He studied and then practiced and practiced. His first magic shows, begun when he was 17, included mostly card tricks. He added new tricks, such as escaping from an ordinary box, once he had perfected them.

3 From those simple beginnings, Houdini's magic tricks became more showy and more daring. He escaped from handcuffs. Then, he allowed audience members to bring their own handcuffs to prove he could escape from *any* pair of handcuffs. Then, he escaped from a straitjacket, hanging upside down by his ankles.

4 How can a performer top his own top performance? Think of a trick that seems truly impossible. Houdini had himself locked into a crate and thrown into a river. He also had himself sealed into a lead coffin, which was placed into a hotel swimming pool. An hour later, Houdini waved to the waiting fans and newspaper reporters.

5 Houdini strongly supported the work of magicians but just as strongly spoke against "fake" magicians who claimed that they had special powers or communicated with "spirits." Houdini would expose these false magicians by visiting their shows and then writing magazine or newspaper articles to reveal how they fooled their audiences.

6 To set himself apart from the "spiritual" magicians, Houdini practiced his tricks, perfected them, and then practiced again. Though Harry Houdini died more than 75 years ago, the man and his tricks have never been matched.

NAME ______________________________

1. The author wrote this article to

   ______ persuade.

   ______ make you laugh.

   ______ give you information.

Write **F** next to each sentence that is a fact. Write **O** next to each sentence that is an opinion.

2. ______ Harry Houdini died more than 75 years ago.

3. ______ Houdini could escape from handcuffs.

4. ______ Harry Houdini was the only "real" magician.

5. ______ Houdini's magic tricks were wonderful.

6. The article gives details about Houdini and his life. Number the details in the order in which the author tells about them.

   ______ He escaped from a straitjacket, hanging upside down.

   ______ Houdini had his first magic shows when he was 17.

   ______ Houdini exposed "fake" magicians.

   ______ Houdini's magic tricks became more showy and daring.

7. Which of these old sayings would Houdini have agreed with?

   ______ Practice makes perfect.

   ______ You are what you eat.

   ______ A watched pot never boils.

8. **Houdini believed he had special powers and could talk to spirits.** Is this statement true or false?

   ____

David Copperfield

What kind of a magician is David Copperfield?

1 An illusion is something that fools the senses or the mind. An illusion may make you think something exists when it really does not. It may be something that appears to be one thing, but is really something else. David Copperfield calls himself an *illusionist*. He is someone who makes or creates illusions.

2 Many people are interested in magic, but most of them are not performing and getting paid for it by age 12. Nor are they teaching college-level classes in magic at age 16. Copperfield was the youngest person ever to be allowed to join the Society of American Magicians. When he got to college himself, Copperfield got the leading part in a play called *The Magic Man*. In addition to acting and singing, he created all the magic in the show. The show ran for longer than any other musical in Chicago's history.

3 Copperfield is a huge success as a showy illusionist, but he has other projects as well. He says that his best work is Project Magic. Copperfield developed a number of tricks done with the hands. These tricks help hospital patients who need to improve their hand strength or coordination to move and control their fingers. Learning to do the tricks also builds confidence. Patients in the program can boast that they can do tricks that able-bodied people can't do.

4 Like many magicians, Copperfield has an interest in the history of magic. He has created a museum and library in which books, articles, and old magic props, or equipment, are stored and displayed. By keeping track of history, Copperfield hopes to save magic for future generations.

NAME ______________________________

1. David Copperfield is an ______________.

2. What did he start doing at age 12?

____

3. What was he doing by age 16?

____

Check all answers that are correct.

4. Which of these words do you think best describe Copperfield?
   ______ thoughtless
   ______ lazy
   ______ hard-working
   ______ talented

5. What do you think a magician could learn from Copperfield's collection of old magic books and equipment?

____

____

6. If you were a magician or an illusionist, what kinds of tricks would you like to do?

____

____

7. The headings below belong in this article. To which paragraph does each heading belong?
   Copperfield's Beginnings ______
   What Is an Illusion? ______
   Saving Magic for the Future ______
   Project Magic ______

8. In your own words, explain what an illusion is.

____

____

9. The youngest person ever to be allowed to join the Society of American Magicians was ______________.

10. Why do you think Copperfield believes that his best work is Project Magic?

____

____

Wiggles Reappears

How do the boys get Wiggles back?

1 "Which word do you think did it?" asked Josh.

2 "What do you mean?" asked Gary, still feeling great because their magic trick had worked. They had finally gotten something to disappear.

3 "Was it *shish-rabbit-ka-zam* or *abra-ca-dab-rabbit*?" Josh asked, working hard to repeat the magic words they had thought up.

4 Gary laughed again, remembering the words. "Oh, I think it was definitely *abra-ca-dab-rabbit*, don't you?"

5 "I don't know," shrugged Josh. "I guess we'll have to try each of them backward to get him back."

6 All of a sudden, it was very quiet. Gary looked at Josh. How in the world were they going to get Wiggles back?

7 "I think I remember all the words," Gary said, trying to encourage Josh. Wiggles was Josh's pet, after all.

8 The boys sat down on the back steps of Josh's house to figure out how to say the words backward so the magic would work the other way.

9 "Okay," said Gary, thinking hard. "We have *zam-ka-rabbit-shish* and *rabbit-dab-ca-abra*."

10 Josh continued, "And *zam-o-rabbit* and just plain old *dabra-ca-abra*."

11 Gary nodded, "I think that's it."

12 *"Ahhhhh!"* The cry came from around the corner of the house. It was Josh's mom.

13 "Mom? What's the matter?" called Josh, as both boys went running.

14 "Now, how many times have I told you not to chew on my..." Josh heard his mom's voice. Just around the corner, both boys stopped short.

15 "Wiggles! He reappeared!" Josh cried.

16 Mom looked at the boys. "Wiggles? Reappeared? Who's going to make my flowers reappear?"

17 The boys looked at each other, smiled, and nodded. They waved their arms and said, in their best magician voices, *"Zam-ka-flowers-SHISH!"*

NAME ______________________________

1. Number the sentences to show the order in which events happened in the story.
   ______ Gary laughed about their magic words.
   ______ The boys heard Josh's mom.
   ______ The boys discovered Mom and Wiggles.
   ______ The boys figured out how to say the words backward.
   ______ Gary felt great because their trick worked.
   ______ The boys tried to make Mom's flowers reappear.

2. What problem do the boys have in this story?

   ____

   ____

3. What problem does Mom have?

   ____

   ____

4. How do the boys try to help Mom? Do you think it will work?

   ____

   ____

   ____

5. Who does Wiggles belong to?

   ____

6. Do you think Wiggles has escaped before? What details in the story helped you answer this question?

   ____

   ____

   ____

7. Do you think the boys will continue working on their magic tricks? Why or why not?

   ____

   ____

   ____

Field Trip

What do the children see during their bus ride?

1 The crisp wind tore at the children. They held their jackets out, letting them puff up with air. The October wind only added to the excitement. Today was a field trip day. The children were in line, being counted before they got onto the rumbling yellow bus. Counting was taking a long time because of the movement of the wind and the children.

2 At last they were on the bus, two to a seat, sometimes three. A few parents spread themselves out and settled in for the noisy, bumpy ride.

3 As the trip began, Mrs. Mason and Steven were playing riddley-riddley-ree in the front seat when Jason tapped their shoulders and pointed. "Oh, look at that neat building!" he cried.

4 Mrs. Mason turned her attention out the window. "This is a little town called *Rockville,*" she said. "It's been here for more than 150 years. Some of those neat buildings are that old."

5 "Wow!" said Steven. "What's in them?"

6 "Well, I see a hardware store, a grocery store, a card shop, a diner..."

7 "And there's a candle shop and a shoe store," added Jason. He, Luisa, and Steven named all the stores they saw. It was easy because there weren't really very many. All of a sudden, the bus was rolling along between tall, dry cornfields waiting to be harvested.

8 "Well," said Jason, "that really was a little town."

9 Riddley-riddley-ree continued, and it was a while before anyone really looked out the window. Riddley-riddley-ree wasn't fair, after all, unless you named something that was inside the bus that everyone could see.

10 When he did look out the window again, Steven saw a long gray wall. It went on and on beside the bus on both sides of the highway. It was so tall that he couldn't see over it. *What could be behind that wall?* Steven wondered.

NAME ______________________

1. The children notice that the town of Rockville is ______________________.

2. What three sights do the children see out the bus window? Write the parts of the sentences from the story that tell you.

____

____

The place where a story happens is the **setting**. An author might describe how a place looks, how it feels, or how it smells. The author of this story described the setting in the first paragraph. Answer these questions.

3. During what time of year does this story take place?

____

4. What kind of day is it?

____

5. What detail tells you that it might be a little chilly?

____

____

6. How do the students feel about the field trip?
   ______ annoyed
   ______ worried
   ______ excited

7. Name one detail from the story that helped you answer question 6.

____

____

8. Write **C** next to the sentence below that is the cause. Write **E** next to the sentence that is the effect.
   ______ No one is really looking out the windows much.
   ______ The students are playing a game.

9. What do you think might be behind the long wall?

____

____

Riddles Along the Way

What ideas do the children have about the wall?

1 "What do you think it's for?" Steven asked Jason and Luisa in the seat behind him. They looked out the bus window where Steven was pointing. They saw the long gray wall that went on like a snake beside them.

2 Luisa had an idea. "Maybe there's a lake on the other side of it," she guessed.

3 "But it's been going on for ages," said Steven. "I didn't think there were any lakes that big around here. Besides, it's on both sides of the road." Jason and Luisa whirled around to the windows on the far side of the bus.

4 "Oh, I guess you're right," Luisa shrugged. "There wouldn't be lakes on both sides of the road, would there?"

5 "Maybe there are castles on both sides of the road," suggested Jason. "And maybe the people who live in the castles built the walls because they don't get along with each other."

6 Steven and Luisa looked at Jason in surprise. Then, Jason smiled and held up a book he'd been reading. Its title was *The Truth about Castles, Knights, and Moats*. Steven and Luisa laughed along with Jason.

7 When he could talk again, Steven said, "For a minute there, I thought you had gone completely nuts."

8 Jason grinned. "Yeah, I could tell." Then, he looked out the window again. "So what do you think it's for?" Mrs. Mason, who had been talking to someone across the aisle, heard the question.

9 "You're wondering about the wall?" she asked. "There are houses on the other side. The wall blocks the highway noise so the people who live there can have a quiet neighborhood."

10 "So my idea was half right," pointed out Jason matter-of-factly. "The people built the walls because they didn't get along with the highway."

NAME ______________________

Write **T** if the sentence is true. Write **F** if the sentence is false.

1. ______ The children saw a castle.

2. ______ The wall was on only one side of the bus.

3. ______ Jason had a book on the bus.

4. ______ The walls surrounded a lake.

5. What does this story tell you about Jason? You may check more than one.
______ He likes to joke around.
______ He is interested in history.
______ He doesn't get along with Steven.
______ He has never been on a field trip before.

6. Do you think Jason is reading a fiction or nonfiction book? How can you tell?

____

____

7. What is the purpose of the long gray wall?

____

____

8. Why do the children decide that there's probably not a lake on the other side of the walls?

____

____

9. What is the author's purpose for writing this story?

____

____

10. Mrs. Mason ______________.
______ knows a lot about the area
______ is too busy to talk to the students
______ probably just moved to the area

One Great Wall

Where is the Great Wall of China, and why was it built?

1 A wall has many uses. It may hold things in. It may keep things out. It may hold things up. In the case of China's Great Wall, the purpose was to keep things out. Tribes of people wanted to move across China's northern mountains and down into China. China's emperors preferred to keep those people out of China. So, four different walls started going up as early as 700 B.C.

2 About 500 years later, the emperor got tired of fighting off the northern tribes. He wanted to connect the four main sections of the wall that had already been built. He sent thousands of peasants, poor people who did not have farms, to work on the wall. Soldiers were there to make sure the peasants stayed and worked. They did work hard, and many of them died.

3 Then, 1,500 years after that, another emperor wanted to make the wall even stronger. He started a program that lasted more than 200 years! The wall got longer, and watch-towers and cannons were added at points all along the length of the wall.

4 In spite of the wall, China did suffer a number of invasions over the years. Still, the wall's size and the human effort that went into it earn it a place on the list of greatest human feats.

The Facts on the Great Wall

Length	1,500 mi.
Width	15–30 ft. at base; 12 ft. at top
Height	25 ft. (average)
Materials	bricks, rocks, packed earth

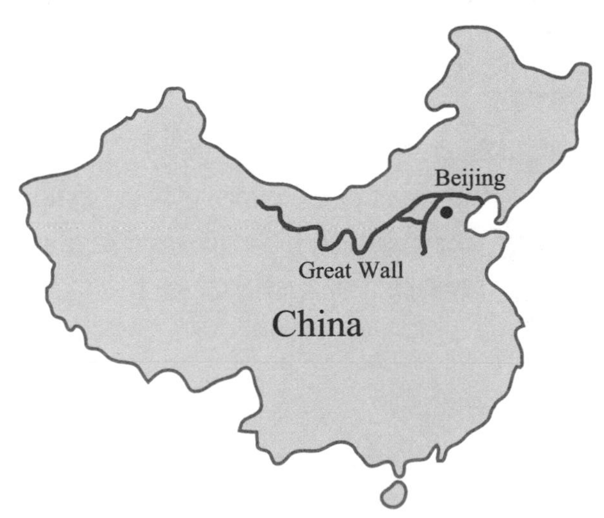

NAME ______________________________

1. The Great Wall of China was built
   ______ as a place for soldiers to live.
   ______ to protect China.
   ______ to honor the emperors.

Write the best word to complete each sentence below.

2. It took hundreds of years to ______________ the Great Wall of China. (move, build, climb)
3. Peasants were poor ______________ who did not have farms. (people, emperors, walls)
4. Today, people may ______________ the Great Wall and walk along it. (twist, visit, hear)
5. What does the map show?

   ____

   ____

6. Based on the map, describe how the Great Wall might look from high above Earth.

   ____

   ____

Write the correct abbreviation in each blank.

mi. ft.

7. If you are standing on the Great Wall, you could be about 25 ______ above the ground.
8. The top of the wall was made 12 ______ wide so soldiers and carts could travel along the wall.
9. If every curve of the wall is measured, it is 1,500 ______ long.
10. If a straight line were drawn from one end of the wall to the other, the line would be 1,200 ______ long.
11. **The Great Wall of China was built by a single emperor.** Is this true or false?

    ____

12. Why do you think watchtowers and cannons were added along the wall?

    ____

13. What else can you think of that is another great human feat?

    ____

A Wall of Names

Why was this wall built?

1 Most walls draw lines between people or things. One wall in Washington, D.C., is meant to invite people to come close. Rather than separate people, it is supposed to draw people together.

2 The low black stone wall that makes up the Vietnam Veterans Memorial stretches along a green grassy slope. The 58,245 names carved into the wall are the names of men and women who died or went missing while serving in the U.S. Armed Forces during the Vietnam War.

3 The committee that was raising money and organizing the memorial held a contest to find a design. They had four requirements. The design for the memorial had to

1. be thoughtful.
2. fit in with its surroundings.
3. contain the names of all those who died during the Vietnam conflict or were still missing.
4. make no political statement about the war.

More than 1,400 design ideas were sent to the committee. From all those ideas, the design of a college student, Maya Ying Lin, was chosen. Construction was completed in 1982.

4 Tens of thousands of people visit the wall each year. Some of them knew people whose names are on the wall. Others visit just to see, and perhaps to remember the 1960s, when Americans hotly disagreed about the war. The wall, though, is not a war memorial, but a memorial to those who served in the war, both living and dead. No matter what one thinks of the Vietnam War, 2.7 million American military people worked hard in difficult conditions, and thousands of them lost their lives. That deserves to be remembered.

NAME ______________________________

1. This article is mostly about
   ______ Maya Ying Lin.
   ______ the Vietnam War.
   ______ the Vietnam Veterans Memorial.

2. The wall was completed in

   ____.

3. How many names are on the wall?

   ____

4. Why was the Vietnam Veterans Memorial built?

   ____

   ____

5. Look at the picture of the wall. Then, look back at the design requirements. Write how you think the wall meets one of those requirements.

   ____

   ____

6. How is the wall different from most walls?

   ____

7. Do you think that holding a contest to find a design for the wall was a good idea? Why or why not?

   ____

   ____

8. The author's purpose for writing this article is
   ______ to entertain.
   ______ to inform.
   ______ to persuade.

9. If you visited the Vietnam Veterans Memorial, how do you think you would feel?

   ____

   ____

A Farm from Long Ago

What will the students learn about at the farm?

1 When the bus stopped, everyone filed out and waited under some large shade trees. Luisa and Steven practiced making wings out of their jackets.

2 "Wow!" said Steven over the wind. "It's even more windy here than it was at school!"

3 Just then, Luisa noticed a woman coming from the big white house. She wore a dress that dragged on the grass. On her head was a small white cap, tied under her chin. Luisa was amazed at how different her own shirt, jeans, and sneakers were from the woman's clothing.

4 Mrs. Mason spoke to the woman for a minute, and then motioned for the students to gather around and listen.

5 "Welcome to Fairfield Farm, children," began the smiling woman. "My name is Mrs. Hoff, and my job is to help you learn about what life was like many years ago."

6 "Hello, Mrs. Hoff," the students echoed.

7 "First, let me tell you a little bit about Fairfield Farm. The Owen family started this farm about 140 years ago. Most of the tools and machines that you will see on the farm today are from the 1860s." Just then, a gust of wind caught Mrs. Hoff's full skirt and nearly pushed her backward. The students giggled.

8 "You will notice," Mrs. Hoff continued, "that life in the 1860s was a little different than it is now. I notice that every time I put this dress on and come to work." Mrs. Hoff grinned, and the students giggled again. "But there are many wonderful things to learn from how farmers and their families lived and worked all those years ago.

9 "Now, I'd like half of you to come with me to the barn first. The rest of you will go with Mrs. Mason to see what's happening in the farm kitchen. Okay?" With a swing of her skirt, Mrs. Hoff set off toward the barn. Luisa and Jason waved to Steven as their groups separated. Luisa crossed her fingers and hoped for lots of animals in the barn.

NAME ______________________________

1. What kind of day is it?

____

2. What are the children going to learn about?

____

____

____

3. How is Luisa's clothing different from Mrs. Hoff's?

____

____

____

4. Have you ever been on a field trip? What kinds of things did you do?

____

____

____

5. Why is Mrs. Hoff dressed in old-fashioned clothing?

____

6. About how old is the farm?
   ______ 100 years old
   ______ 140 years old
   ______ 160 years old

7. Is this story realistic? Why or why not?

____

8. What is the setting for this story?

____

9. What do you think will happen next?

____

____

____

In the Barn

What do the students learn about in the barn?

1 Luisa could hear the noises even before they got to the barn. There were definitely animals in there.

2 "Jason, do you think we'll see cows, horses, or what?" she asked excitedly.

3 "I'm hoping for geese, myself," answered Jason. He flapped his arms and made a honking sound.

4 When they stepped into the barn, Luisa saw a man standing by a fence talking to some animals. *Excellent!* thought Luisa, *I forgot about sheep!* The man had on an old brown hat, a light brown shirt, brown pants, and heavy brown boots.

5 "Hello, Mr. Brown. How are you today?" Mrs. Hoff sang out.

6 Luisa giggled. *Well, what else could his name be?* she thought to herself.

7 The man touched his hat in an old-fashioned way to greet Mrs. Hoff.

8 "I was just checking to see how the wool was growing," said Mr. Brown.

9 "Does wool really grow?" asked one of the students.

10 "Why, sure it does," Mr. Brown replied. "I clipped these sheep just about down to the skin in spring. Now just look how woolly they are. By next spring, they'll have a nice crop of wool for me to clip off again."

11 Jason had a question. "What happens to it then?"

12 Mr. Brown marked off the steps on his fingers. "First, the wool gets washed. Then, it gets cleaned and fluffed, or carded, then dyed. Next, the wool gets spun into yarn. Then, someone weaves it into cloth. In fact, these clothes I'm wearing are made of wool from these very sheep."

13 Luisa couldn't wait any more. "Do the sheep have names?"

14 "Oh, yes," said Mr. Brown, turning toward the sheep. "This is Socks. This is Pants. There's Shirt. Over here is Yarn, and this one is Coat."

15 Luisa caught the twinkle in Mr. Brown's eyes and smiled at him. *Well, what else could their names be?*

NAME ______________________________

1. In the barn, the students saw

____.

In this story, the author uses **dialogue** to move the story along. For each piece of dialogue below, fill in the name of the character who said it. Then, write what the dialogue tells you about the character or the story.

2. "I was just checking to see how the wool was growing."

____

3. "Does wool really grow?"

____

4. "I clipped these sheep just about down to the skin in spring."

____

5. Write **R** next to the sentences that tell about something real. Write **M** next to the sentences that are about made-up things.

   ______ Farmers raise sheep.
   ______ A sheep's coat is wool.
   ______ Sheep come in many bright colors, just like yarn.

6. Number the sentences to show the order in which wool is processed.

   ______ Card the wool.
   ______ Weave the wool.
   ______ Clip the wool.
   ______ Spin the wool.
   ______ Wash the wool.
   ______ Dye the wool.

7. Why is Mr. Brown's name funny to Luisa?

____

8. What material is Mr. Brown's clothes made of?

____

____

9. **Then, someone weaves it into cloth.** Is this statement a fact or an opinion?

____

In the Kitchen

What does Steven learn in the kitchen?

1 Steven couldn't believe the smell coming from the kitchen as he walked across the back porch. It was great.

2 Mrs. Mason held the squeaky screen door open. Steven and the rest of the group went through it. *Ahhh,* thought Steven, *fresh bread!*

3 Inside the big square kitchen was an old wooden table. On the far side was a huge stove. Above it was a round pipe going up and then out through the wall. A woman dressed almost like Mrs. Hoff was standing behind the table. There was one difference though. This woman had her sleeves rolled up. It was hot in this kitchen. The woman began talking just as if the group had been there all along.

4 "When the Owens ran this farm in the 1860s, Saturday would have been bread-baking day. A farm wife baked a week's worth of bread for her family and any hired hands who lived at the farm." While she talked, she kept right on pulling and pushing a huge mound of bread dough on the table.

5 "Did anyone notice that it's rather warm in here?" the woman asked.

6 "I sure did!" answered Steven right away. His classmates nodded their heads.

7 "That's one of the reasons a farm wife baked bread only once a week. It's quite a process, and it means that the kitchen is really going to heat up," explained the woman. She brushed some hair back with her arm.

8 "Speaking of heat, the stove is hungry again." She looked up at the students. "Would each of you go and get a piece of wood from the porch to fill my wood box? Then, we'll slice one of these loaves and see how the bread turned out. Okay?"

9 *With pleasure,* thought Steven, and he led the way out to the woodpile on the porch.

NAME ______________________

1. It's hot in the kitchen because

______________________________.

2. What does the woman mean when she says, "The stove is hungry"?

____

____

3. Is Steven eager to taste the bread? How can you tell?

____

____

Write **F** next to each sentence that is a fact. Write **O** next to each sentence that is an opinion.

4. ______ Some people still bake their own bread.

5. ______ Bread is best when baked in a wood stove.

6. ______ All bread smells good when it's baking.

7. Why did farm wives bake bread only once a week?

____

____

8. After they fill up the wood box, what will the students do next?

______ get back on the bus

______ start a fire

______ sample the bread

9. On the farm in the 1860s, Saturday was ______________________.

10. Have you ever baked something from scratch before? Tell about it.

____

____

____

____

Baking Bread

Read to see what this newspaper article has to say about baking bread.

Baking Today

1 You may think that baking bread is a lost art. For one local woman, though, it is a daily event. Evelyn Seeley is the retired owner of A Loaf a Day bakery. Now that her grown children are running the bakery, Seeley has time to follow her own interests.

2 And what are her interests? Bread, of course! Almost every day, Seeley bakes a different kind of bread. She finds recipes among her many cookbooks, or she searches for them on her computer. "With the computer now, I don't think I'll ever run out of recipes," says Seeley. She doesn't think that she has repeated a recipe in her two years of retirement.

3 Seeley offers this recipe for our readers today. She says, "It's an oldie but a goody." Try it for yourself and see.

Sally Lunn Yeast Bread

1 pkg. dry yeast

$\frac{1}{4}$ c. warm water

6 T. butter

2 T. plus 1 tsp. sugar

2 eggs

$\frac{3}{4}$ c. milk

3 c. flour

$1\frac{1}{2}$ tsp. salt

4 Sprinkle yeast into the lukewarm water and set aside. In a bowl, cream butter and sugar. Beat in eggs. Blend in milk alternately with flour and salt. Beat after each addition. Then, add water and yeast. Beat until very smooth. Cover bowl and set in warm place. Let rise until double in bulk. Beat down with a wooden spoon and pour batter into a greased 9-in. tube pan. Let rise until just above edge of pan. Bake in preheated 350° F oven for 40–45 min.

NAME ______________________________

1. What did Evelyn Seeley do before she retired?

____

2. What does she do now that she's retired?

____

3. Number the sentences to show the order of the steps in the bread recipe.

______ Add eggs.
______ Let rise.
______ Add milk, flour, and salt.
______ Put yeast in water.
______ Add yeast.
______ Cream butter and sugar.

4. What type of selection is this?

______ a biography
______ a newspaper article
______ a short story

Recipes often use short forms, or **abbreviations**, of words. Look at the common recipe words in the box. Write each word next to the correct item from the recipe.

cups	**package**
Fahrenheit	**tablespoons**
minutes	**teaspoons**

5. 40–45 min. ______________________________

6. 6 T. butter ______________________________

7. 350° F ______________________________

8. 3 c. flour ______________________________

9. 1 pkg. dry yeast ______________________________

10. $1\frac{1}{2}$ tsp. salt ______________________________

11. Does the photo add anything to the article? Explain.

____

____

12. Why does Seeley think she'll never run out of recipes now?

____

13. Who runs Seeley's bakery today?

____

All About the Farm

What did the students like best about the farm?

1 "Jason! Did you see those geese?" Steven called to his friend as they got near the bus. The two boys had been in different groups during the class field trip. Now, it was time to get on the bus and head back to school.

2 Jason waved to his friend. "I sure did. They were huge. One of them came right up to me, and he was as tall as my shoulder." Jason had really enjoyed the geese, and everyone around him could tell.

3 "I think they were my favorite, too," said Steven, as he and Jason slid into a seat. In front of them, Luisa was telling Mrs. Mason about the sheep. "They were so fuzzy. Did you feel them?" Luisa wiggled her fingers in the air as if she were curling them into the sheep's wool.

4 Mrs. Mason laughed. "I know what you mean, Luisa. It made me want to curl up inside the pen with the sheep."

5 Steven nodded. "I think the sheep might have been my favorite, too, Luisa."

6 "What about you, Mrs. Mason?" asked Luisa. "What was your favorite part?"

7 "Oh, I loved all of it," she said, shaking her head. "If I had to pick just one thing, though, I would say... the bread..."

8 "Oh, the bread," broke in Jason as he hugged his stomach. "It was so warm."

9 "And sweet," added Luisa.

10 Everyone looked at Steven to get his reaction. He had a sort of dreamy smile on his face. "It was...perfect," was all he said.

NAME ______________________________

1. This story is mostly about
   ______ what the students learned on their field trip.
   ______ what the students liked best about the field trip.
   ______ how much Jason liked the geese.

2. What is Luisa's favorite part about the farm?

   ____

   ____

3. Which student seems unsure about his favorite part?

   ____

   ____

4. How can you tell?

   ____

   ____

5. Would you say that Steven is hard to please or easy to please? Explain.

   ____

   ____

   ____

6. Where are the characters when they have this conversation?
   ______ in the barn
   ______ in the kitchen
   ______ on the bus
   ______ outside

7. Write **first**, **next**, and **last** to tell in what order the events below happened.
   ____________ Steven had a dreamy look on his face.
   ____________ Steven and Jason got on the bus.
   ____________ Mrs. Mason said she liked the bread best.

8. Do you think Mrs. Mason really wanted to curl up in the pen with the sheep? Why or why not?

   ____

   ____

   ____

Caught in Traffic

What happens on the way back from the field trip?

1 Jason was winning. He and his friends had been trying to see who could list the most cool things that they had seen on the field trip. Jason had 27 so far. Steven was starting to catch up, though.

2 As Luisa thought up more ideas, she gazed out the bus window and realized that the bus wasn't moving. She saw long lines of cars beside them and stretching around a curve in front of them.

3 "Hey, I wonder what's happening," she said, pointing out the window. "Everyone is stopped."

4 The bus driver heard Luisa and nodded his head. "This often happens on the outer edges of the city, especially on Friday afternoons. Everyone has to be somewhere, and right now they're all right here," he said, turning to frown, but in a friendly way, at Luisa.

5 Jason was a little worried. "What if we don't get back to school on time?"

6 "Oh, we have plenty of time," Mrs. Mason quickly assured him. "And if it does get late, the bus driver can radio the school and let them know what's happening. It'll be all right."

7 "Just look at them all," said Luisa, still gazing out the window. "How many do you think there are?"

8 "Let's see!" suggested Steven. "One, two, three, four, five, six, seven, eight…."

9 "Okay, okay," cut in Luisa, waving a hand at Steven, "that's annoying." She grinned at Steven, and Steven grinned right back.

10 Jason had a different thought. "I wonder where they're all going and where they came from." The three friends all looked out the window at the cars disappearing into the distance. Each of them wondered about all the different kinds of people and all of their different reasons for being here right now, clogging up the highway.

NAME ______________________

Write the best word to complete each sentence below.

1. Up ahead, the line of cars went around a ______________.
   (curve, ledge, movement)
2. Jason was worried about the bus being ______________. (hard, late, extra)
3. Steven wanted to ______________ the cars. (spin, read, count)
4. Have you ever been stuck in traffic? Write about how it felt.

   ____
   ____
   ____
   ____

5. What might cause a traffic jam? List as many reasons as you can.

   ____
   ____
   ____

6. How do you think the bus driver feels about the traffic jam?
   _____ amused
   _____ joyful
   _____ frustrated
7. If the bus is late, what will the bus driver do?

   ____
   ____

8. Write **C** next to the sentence below that is the cause. Write **E** next to the sentence that is the effect.

   _____ Lots of cars are on the highway at the same time.

   _____ The cars are causing a traffic jam.

How Many Are There?

Read to see why we count things.

1 Look in any newspaper and you are likely to see numbers. We like to know how many inches of rain we've had, or how many students are in our schools. We want to know how much the city government is spending, or how many people have voted. We like to see numbers.

2 Fortunately, many people like to count or keep track of things. They count traffic accidents and help us decide where to put stop signs and traffic lights. They count people to help us decide when we need more houses or more schools. They count how many people catch the flu and tell us when to get shots.

3 Some numbers help us see that we need to change something. Other numbers show how things are changing. The numbers in the graph on this page show how the population and the number of cars in the United States have changed. How has the growth in population affected or changed the United States? How has the increase in the number of cars affected the country? Think about how this growth has affected you and your community.

Population and Number of Cars in the United States (1970–2010)

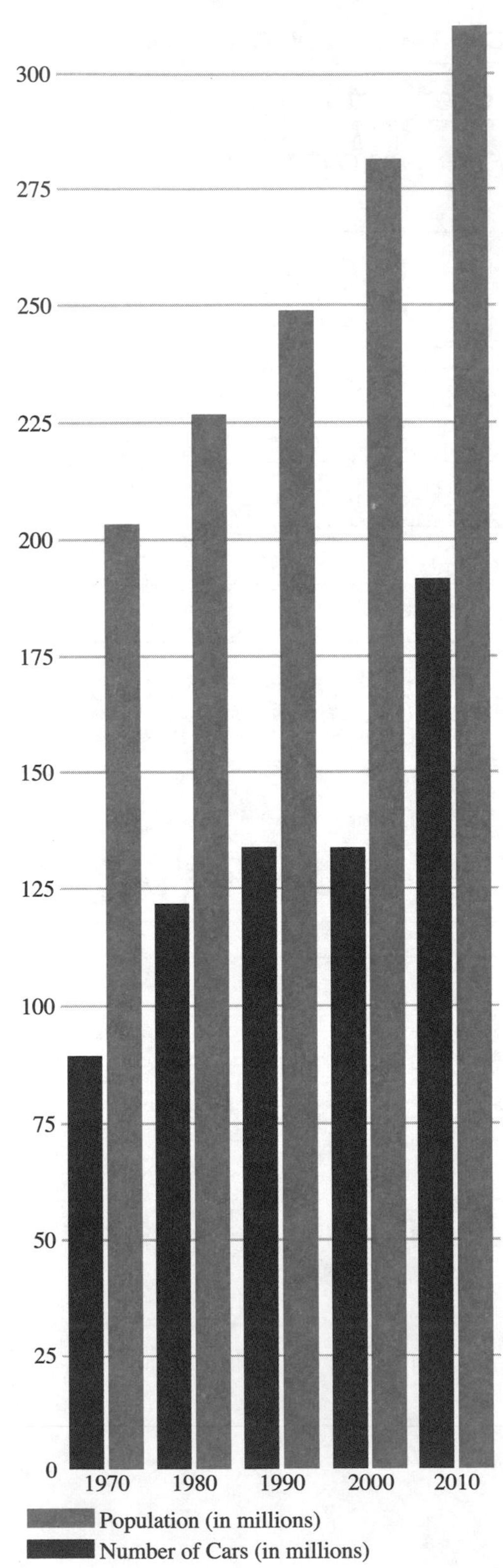

NAME ______________________

1. What kinds of things do we count? List two examples from the article.

____

2. What do we learn from counting things?

____

____

3. How do you think the information shown in this graph affects you and your community?

____

____

4. What can the number of traffic accidents tell us?

____

____

5. How many years does this chart cover?

____

6. Why is the title of the chart important?

____

Use the bar graph to answer these questions.

7. For each year, which is greater, the population or the number of cars?

____

8. If you want population data for 1950, would this graph help you? How can you tell?

____

____

9. What was the population of the United States in 1970?

____

10. How many cars were there in 1990?

____

Sidewalk Art

How do a sister and brother fill a long, hot afternoon?

1 I feel like a cactus. No, that's too dry. I feel like the glass greenhouse at the city park, all steamy and cloudy inside because the plants like it warm and moist. I feel like…

2 Oh, it's no use. I don't feel like anything. I'm just hot. It's hot outside. It's hot inside. There is nothing to do. I sit on the front steps of our building, trying to stay in a small triangle of shade. At the same time, I try to touch as little of the step as possible because everything feels hot and sticky, including my own skin.

3 I squint toward the sun to make bright, fuzzy patterns with my eyelashes. I watch a tree across the street. I can count on the fingers of one hand the number of leaves moving in the breeze. That's how weak the breeze is.

4 I try to think of something to do. I give myself a deadline. When the shade of my building gets to that crack in the sidewalk, I will do something. It happens slowly, just like everything else in the heat. When it gets close, I go down to the crack and watch. Yes, it's time. What should I do?

5 My brother Fujio's box of chalk is sitting forgotten at the bottom of the steps. I take out a piece of yellow chalk and make a blazing sun on the sidewalk. I surround it with white, then with every color in the chalk box.

6 Fujio appears at my side. "What's that, Tatsu?" he asks.

7 I don't say anything, but I write "Heat" at the bottom of my drawing. He just shrugs. Then, he gets the black chalk (his favorite color) and starts coloring. He fills a whole square of the sidewalk.

8 "What's that?" I ask.

9 "Shade," he says.

10 "Fujio, that's not…," I begin to say, but then I stop. It doesn't really matter. It's something to do, and that's a bonus on a hot day.

NAME ______________________________

1. Tatsu is sitting in the shade on the front steps because

____.

2. Tatsu titles her drawing "Heat" because

____

____.

3. Write **R** next to the sentences that tell about something real. Write **M** next to the sentences that are about made-up things.

______ A person can make shade by drawing a picture of it.

______ A person can draw a picture of heat.

______ A person can draw a picture of the sun.

The **narrator** is the person who tells a story. Answer these questions.

4. Because the narrator is also a character, she uses the words *I* and *me* to tell her story. Find a place in the story where one of these words is used. Write the sentence here.

____

____

5. Where in the story do you discover what the narrator's name is?

____

6. Do you think Tatsu and Fujio live in the city, in the country, or in a small town? Why?

____

____

7. From whose point of view is the story told?

______ Tatsu's ______ Fujio's ______ Not enough information is given.

8. The author uses lots of descriptions to tell how hot it is. List three details from the story that help you imagine the heat.

____

____

____

9. What do you like to do on a super hot summer day?

____

Wishes on the Sidewalk

How do the children try to cool themselves off?

1 It's late afternoon now, and it's getting a little better. The heat, I mean. The shade came around to the front of the building, so at least the sidewalk doesn't burn you anymore.

2 I tease Fujio about drawing a picture of shade. He's pretty cool about it. He just says, "It helped me think about not being hot."

3 I look at my own picture of the hot, hot sun. Maybe I should have tried it Fujio's way. Maybe my sun picture just makes it hotter here.

4 I see our neighbors Mario and Katie coming down the sidewalk. They stop and look at our pictures. Mario points at Fujio's black square and raises his eyebrows.

5 "Shade," sighs Fujio, as if he is tired of being an artist who is not understood. Mario wrinkles his brow for a moment, and then bends down and picks up the blue chalk. He begins at a corner, just like Fujio did, and covers a square with blue.

6 It's too hot to talk, so we just wait. We figure he'll explain. When Mario is done, he stands up and gives a little bow. "Cool water," he says. Fujio and I smile. Then, Katie jumps up and grabs the white chalk.

7 "Watch this, Tatsu," she says to me. Mario steps aside as Katie begins in the middle of a square. The square fills with white as the chalk gets smaller and smaller.

8 Finally, she stands. "A snow bank," she announces.

9 Fujio, Mario, and I cheer and clap. "Bravo! Bravo!"

10 Katie sits back down on the steps and leans back. I can tell she and the boys are thinking cool thoughts. I get up and make a big black "X" across my hot sun picture. Then, I go and sit right in the middle of Katie's snow bank. It's so cool it doesn't even melt.

NAME ______________________________

1. Why do Mario and Katie choose to draw pictures of cool water and a snow bank?

____

____

2. Why does Tatsu cross out her own picture of the sun?

____

____

3. Which word best describes the group of friends?
   ______ energetic
   ______ creative
   ______ anxious

4. Mario doesn't use words to ask Fujio what he drew. How does he ask instead?

____

5. What is the author's purpose in writing this story?
   ______ to teach   ______ to persuade   ______ to entertain

6. Why is the story titled "Wishes on the Sidewalk"?

____

____

____

7. Do you think that thinking about cool things can help a person cool down? Write why or why not.

____

____

____

8. Can you remember a hot day? How did it feel? Describe it so that someone else can imagine it easily.

____

____

____

Drawings on the Wall

What might you have been doing if you lived 17,000 years ago?

1 The year, if anyone were counting, would be around 15,000 B.C. You were probably looking for food, maybe using an animal skin to carry water, and possibly tending a fire to keep warm. Oh, and there's one other thing. You might have been drawing pictures on the walls of your cave.

2 We don't know why you drew the pictures. You had to go deep into the cave to do it, so you must have had a plan. You probably took a lamp made out of animal fat with you. Some of us think you drew pictures to bring good luck when you hunted. Others think the spears in some of the pictures mean that you were teaching other people to hunt.

3 For paint, you mixed animal fat with various things, such as dirt or berries. You used the ragged end of a stick to brush or dab the paint onto the wall. Sometimes, you didn't feel like using any color and you used the end of a stick that had been burned in the fire. It made broad black marks, much like modern artists make with chalk.

4 You drew what you saw around you—animals such as buffalo, deer, horses, and sometimes birds and fish. You drew people, but not very often. Sometimes, you made handprints or basic shape patterns on the wall.

5 You'll be happy to know that we think your pictures are really quite good. The buffalo look strong and powerful. And many of the horses and deer look graceful. You drew their shapes well.

6 We have found your drawings in more than 130 caves, mostly in France and England. We wonder if there are more that we haven't found yet. We wonder so many things, but we'll just have to satisfy ourselves with admiring your drawings. We're glad you made them.

NAME ___________________________

1. This article is mostly about
   ______ animals that lived thousands of years ago.
   ______ early cave art.
   ______ how early people survived.

2. What did early cave artists use for paint?

   ____

3. Where did early artists make their drawings?

   ____

4. Early cave art has been found in more than ________ caves.

5. How do you like the cave art shown on this page? How is it the same or different from other drawings you have seen of mammoths?

   ____

   ____

   ____

6. Who is the author addressing, or talking to, in this article?
   ______ the reader
   ______ the people who made the cave paintings
   ______ artists of today

7. Why is this an unusual way to write the article?

   ____

   ____

   ____

8. Most of the cave drawings have been found in _______________ and _______________.

9. What is the main idea of paragraph 4?

   ____

   ____

10. About how many years ago were the cave paintings made?

   ____

Roman Wall Art

Read to see what Romans put on their walls.

1 Do you have pictures all over the walls of your home? If you don't, maybe you would like to. How about a scene from an old, famous story? Or maybe you would like a picture of a famous world leader having a meeting with other important people.

2 If you had lived in Rome about 2,000 years ago, you could have had pictures like these on a wall in your home. I don't mean just "on" a wall. I mean the whole wall could have been the picture.

3 Romans would often create sculptures on the sides of their buildings, near the top. These sculptures, called **bas-relief**, would be raised out of the flat exterior wall. This would create the illusion of the sculptures coming out of the background.

4 An artwork that covers a wall is a **mural**. *Mural* comes from *murus*, the Latin word for "wall." That seems fitting because the Romans (who spoke Latin) were great muralists. Some of their murals showed characters from Rome's many **myths**, or traditional stories. Other scenes showed important historical events. And others showed common events. One mural that still exists shows a bakery. In front, customers wait in line. The baker stands behind a counter, and behind him are bakery supplies. The mural gives us much information about the Rome of 2,000 years ago.

5 Sometimes, instead of painting a mural, Romans used an art form called **mosaic**. A mosaic is a picture formed by tiles, or tiny pieces of glass or pottery. The pieces are arranged, and then held in place with glue or something similar to cement. One Roman mosaic is so large that it is made up of about a million tiny tiles. The size of this mosaic tells us that the person who owned the home was either very important, very wealthy, or both.

6 What if murals for our homes were still popular? What pictures do you suppose would be on the walls at your house? And what might people 2,000 years from now learn about your family and your world from those pictures?

NAME ______________________

1. Would you like to have a mural in your home? Write why or why not.

____

____

2. Do you think the author wrote this article to make you laugh, give you information, or persuade you to do something?

____

3. The author included some bold words in the article. He wanted readers to learn those words, so he included their meanings nearby. Find one of the words and look for its meaning. Write the word and its meaning here.

____

____

Write the best word to complete each sentence below.

4. I would like a ______________ of a garden on my wall. (jacket, picture, notebook)

5. The bread in the Roman ______________ mural looks yummy. (bakery, crown, sticky)

6. Would you like to use a million tiny ______________ to make a mosaic? (pieces, motions, signs)

7. Write **T** for **true** or **F** for **false** next to each statement below.
   ______ Romans created sculptures on the sides of their buildings.
   ______ A mosaic is carved into a stone wall.
   ______ Murals do not tell us much about the ancient Romans.
   ______ Myths are traditional stories.

8. What is paragraph 4 mostly about?

____

9. What kind of artwork hangs on the walls of your home? What does it say about your family?

____

____

____

____

From Lucy

What does Lucy share with her pen pal?

Dear Isabel,

1 First, I have to say that I just love your name. When my teacher was assigning pen pals, I hoped I would get you, and I did. I'm glad our teachers were pen pals when they were younger, because now we get to be pen pals.

2 I am Lucy. My name is really Lucinda, but no one ever calls me that. I am the only person in the whole third grade with red hair. I pretend that I don't like it, but secretly I don't mind. It sets me apart from the crowd. Mom says it's easy to spot me in the third-grade choir.

3 I have a mother, a father, and a little brother. My dad plans houses for people. Sometimes he works at his office, and sometimes he works at home. Mom takes care of us. She also paints things, like flower pots and little signs for people's gardens, and sells them. My little brother plays with trucks. That's pretty much all he does.

4 The neatest thing we did this summer was go to the beach. It was my first trip to the ocean. We drove all day from West Virginia to South Carolina and stayed in a hotel not too far from the beach. I loved the sand! We walked all along the shore and found pretty stones and little sea creatures that I had never seen before. I'll never forget the sound of the waves as they rolled and rolled into the beach.

5 Do you realize that it's possible that you and I have touched the same water? My teacher says that currents in the ocean keep it moving all the time. Maybe the water on the beach in South Carolina had come from the Dominican Republic.

6 I know that's kind of a goofy idea, but it helps me to think that we're not very far away from each other. I hope you can write back soon. I am eager to hear all about you and your family.

Your pen pal,
Lucy

NAME ______________________________

1. The members of Lucy's family are

____.

2. What is Lucy's real name?

____

3. Where does Lucy's pen pal live? How do you know?

____

____

4. What details do we learn about Lucy from her letter?

____

____

5. What do you think will happen after Lucy finishes writing her letter?

____

____

6. How do Lucy's teacher and Isabel's teacher know each other?

____

____

7. What makes Lucy feel closer to Isabel?

____

____

8. What is paragraph 4 of Lucy's letter mostly about?

____

____

9. If you had a pen pal, what important details would you share about yourself?

____

____

____

At the Shore

Read to see what's at the beach and why.

The Beach

1 When you close your eyes and imagine a beach, what do you see? Do you see steep cliffs and rocks washed by waves? Or do you see a long strip of gleaming sand, with waves gently lapping at the edges? Both pictures are correct. It just depends where on Earth you are standing.

2 In addition to sandy beaches and rocky beaches, many other beaches are covered with gravel or stones that would be unpleasant or difficult to walk on. One thing is common among beaches, though. They all have some kind of rock or stone material. Why?

3 It starts with the constant motion of water against a shore. Soil and plant material get washed away. Then, add wind, rain, and frost, which all work with the water to break down solid rock into smaller pieces. The temperature, the strength of the waves, and the type of rock all affect how quickly, or slowly, the rock breaks down.

The Waves

4 Now, what about those waves? If you've been to the shore, you've seen them. They can nibble at your toes in the sand, or they can be loud and crashing and dangerous. You can blame the wind.

5 When the wind blows over the ocean or even a lake, it gives some of its energy to the water. The water, in turn, moves. The hard part to understand is that a wave does not move forward across the surface. The water in a wave moves up and down. Think of how a rug acts when you shake it. A wave appears to roll along the surface of the rug, but any point on that rug moves only up and down, not forward.

6 The next time you are on a beach, think about all these processes—the water and wind, the rain and frost. Without them, there would be no beach.

NAME ______________________

1. What do all beaches have in common?

2. Why do beaches have stones or sand on them?

3. What causes waves?

4. Why does the article mention a rug?

5. This article has two sections. What are they titled?

6. If you were especially interested in water, what section would you look under?

7. "They can nibble at your toes in the sand, or they can be loud and crashing and dangerous." What is the author describing?

8. What forces work together to break down rock into smaller pieces?

9. Is this selection fiction or nonfiction?

10. Have you ever been to the beach? If so, describe it. If not, tell about what kind of beach you would like to visit.

From Isabel

What does Isabel write in reply to her pen pal's letter?

Dear Lucy,

1 I think Lucinda is very pretty. But Lucy seems very friendly, so I will stay with Lucy. I loved getting your letter. I never knew anyone with red hair before.

2 I am Isabel. You already know that, I guess. I have long black hair. My mother says it looks green when the sun shines on it. I think she is just kidding, though.

3 You are so lucky to have a little brother. I have four sisters! They are all older than I am, and they all think they can tell me what to do. If I had a younger brother (or sister), I would never be bossy.

4 Maybe our fathers should work together! Your father plans houses, and my father builds houses. Maybe they should build one in South Carolina, and we could meet there. What do you think?

5 My mama takes care of us, too. She is the best cook in the world. Papa always says that it's good he has to work for a living. Otherwise, he would sit around and eat all day!

6 I am glad you like the beach. Here on my island, it would be a sad thing if someone didn't like the beach. Sometimes, when Papa comes home early from work, we take picnics to the beach. If we stay after dark, Papa plays his guitar. Those are the best days. The next time you see the moon, think of me and Mama dancing on the beach in its light.

Your pen pal,
Isabel

NAME ____________________

Isabel wrote a friendly letter to her pen pal. She began the letter with "Dear Lucy." That is the **greeting**. She ended her letter with "Your pen pal, Isabel." That is the **closing** of the letter.

1. Suppose you are writing a letter. Write the greeting of your letter here. Remember to put a comma after your greeting.

   ____

2. Now, write the closing of your letter. Note that there is a comma between the closing words and your name.

   ____

Write **T** if the sentence is **true**. Write **F** if the sentence is **false**.

3. ______ Isabel is the oldest child in her family.
4. ______ Isabel's father makes his living by playing guitar.
5. ______ Isabel thinks her mother is a good cook.
6. ______ Isabel sometimes feels bossed around by her sisters.
7. Name three things that Isabel and Lucy have in common.

   ____

   ____

8. What does Isabel say Lucy should do the next time she sees the moon?

   ____

   ____

9. **The Dominican Republic is an island.** Is this true or false? How do you know?

   ____

10. If you were writing a letter back to Isabel, what would you want to ask her about her life?

   ____

   ____

   ____

The Dominican Republic

Read to find out about this small island nation.

Where Is It?

1 South of Florida, a string of islands dots the ocean. One of them is Hispaniola (*hiss pan YO la*). Its name points to the fact that Christopher Columbus visited the island in 1492. As a result, Spain ruled the island for the next 300 years. Two nations now share the island. Haiti makes up the western third. The Dominican Republic makes up the eastern two-thirds.

How Big Is It?

2 The Dominican Republic's area is about 18,000 square miles. That's about the same size as Connecticut and Rhode Island combined. The island's population of 8 million, however, is about twice the population of those two states.

What Happens There?

3 Most people live close to the island's coast. Most of the cities are there, and so is the best farmland. Sugar cane has been the island's most important crop for hundreds of years. The mountainous interior is split by deep valleys where farmers raise cattle.

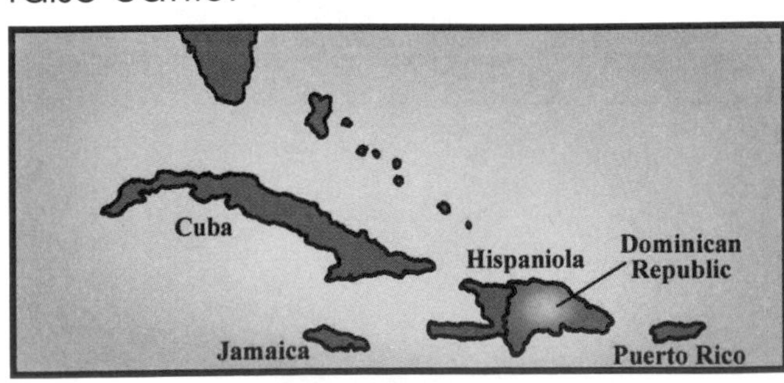

What Is There to Do?

4 Like many other tropical islands, the Dominican Republic views tourism as an important industry. The coastal cities, especially, depend on tourists to fill their hotels and restaurants. The natural beauty of the beaches and of the forest regions draw Dominicans and tourists alike.

5 When you're ready for something else, wander into town to see local craftspeople and artists and their wares. If you like parades and costumes, go in February for Carnival. Music, dancing, and people in colorful masks will greet you at nearly every street corner. Whether you go to join the crowds or to get away from the crowds, there will be a place for you in the Dominican Republic.

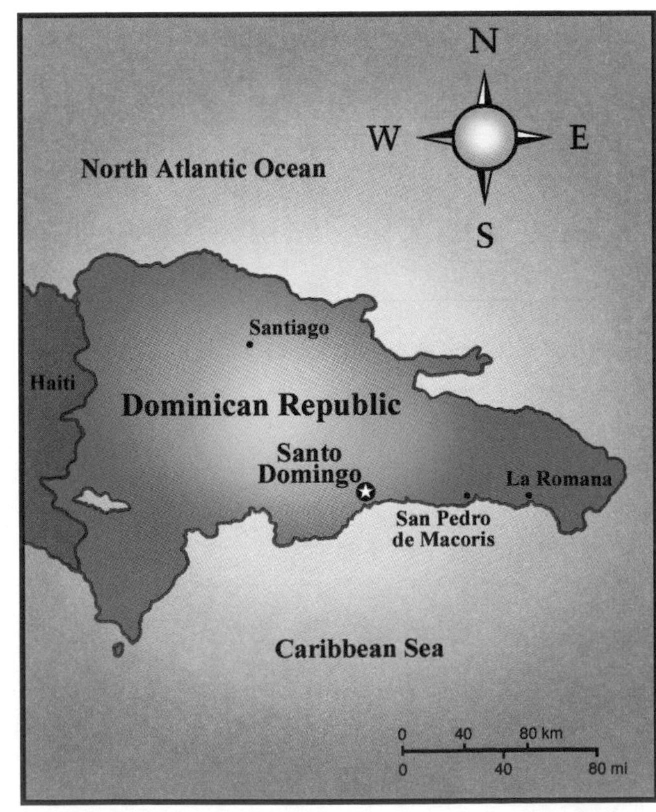

NAME ______________________________

1. The Dominican Republic is about as big as ____________ and ____________ combined.

2. Which population is larger---the Dominican Republic's or Connecticut and Rhode Island's?

____

3. What does the article say about the Dominican Republic's weather?

____

4. What do you know about the weather in Connecticut and Rhode Island? How would it compare to the Dominican Republic's weather?

____

____

5. If the author wanted to add this sentence to the article, under what heading should it go?

   Workers also harvest valuable lumber from the coastal forests.

____

6. If you need a quick reminder about the location of the island, under what heading should you look?

____

Look at the map to answer these questions.

7. Which city is the capital? How can you tell?

____

____

8. What city is farther north than the others?

____

9. What country lies to the west of the Dominican Republic?

____

10. Why is February a good time to visit the Dominican Republic?

____

____

Lucy and Isabel: Pen Pals

How are Lucy and her pen pal the same and different?

1 "Mom! I just got a letter from my pen pal," called Lucy when her mom walked in the door.

2 Mrs. Teeman smiled. "Oh, good! Maybe you won't have to camp out beside the mailbox anymore," she teased Lucy. "Tell me all about it while we unpack the groceries."

3 "Okay," said Lucy, pulling fruit out of a bag. "We have a lot in common. She likes to go to the beach, too. Can you imagine dancing under the stars?" Lucy twirled around with a bunch of bananas for a partner.

4 Mrs. Teeman laughed at Lucy's excitement. "Hmm, sounds nice. What else does she say?" she asked.

5 "Oh, our dads are both in the house-building business," Lucy chattered on. "Isabel thinks they should build a house in South Carolina. Then, we could meet at the beach for vacation."

6 "Sounds like a dreamy vacation," commented Mrs. Teeman from inside the refrigerator.

7 Lucy paused thoughtfully over a box of spaghetti. "Of course, we're different in some ways, too."

8 "Well, that's natural," Mrs. Teeman assured Lucy. "In what ways?"

9 "The biggest difference is that Isabel has four older sisters." Lucy made a face as she went on. "She says she wants a little brother or sister."

10 "Did you tell her about having a little brother?" asked Mrs. Teeman.

11 Lucy nodded and said, "Isabel says she would never be bossy."

12 "That sounds like a good plan," said Mrs. Teeman, with a motherly glance.

13 "And," continued Lucy, "she says her mother is a great cook."

14 Mrs. Teeman looked crushed. "That's different from your life?"

15 Lucy realized that what she had said hadn't come out quite right. "Oh," she said quickly, "that's one of the ways Isabel and I are the same." Lucy gave her mother a quick hug and made a hasty exit. "I better go answer Isabel's letter."

NAME ______________________________

1. Lucy is excited because ______________________________.

2. Lucy's mother is just returning from ______________________________.

3. Does Lucy seem helpful or selfish in this story? Give reasons for your answer.

____

Lucy notices that she and her pen pal, Isabel, are alike in some ways and different in others. Help her compare. Write what is the same about both girls in the space provided. Then, write what is different about each girl.

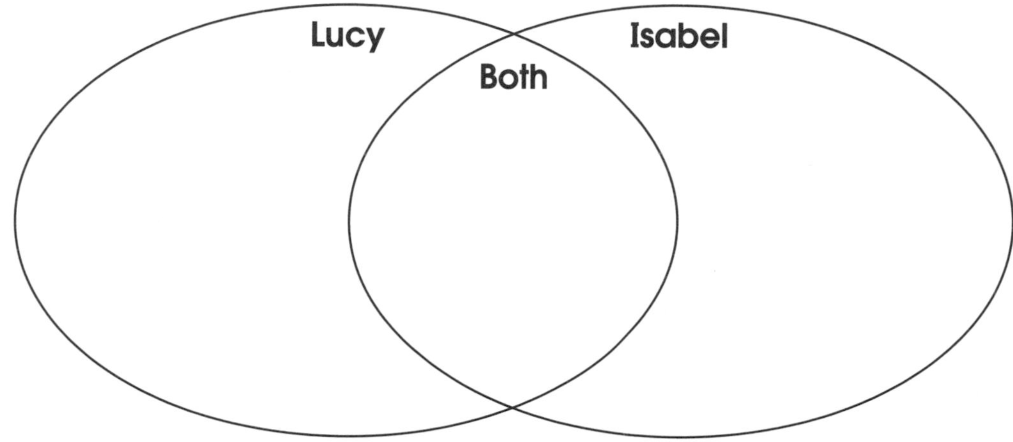

4. Choose one piece of dialogue from the story, and write it on the line. Tell what the dialogue tells you about the character or the story.

____

____

5. In paragraph 14, why does Mrs. Teeman look crushed?

____

6. Write **C** next to the sentence below that is the cause. Write **E** next to the sentence that is the effect.

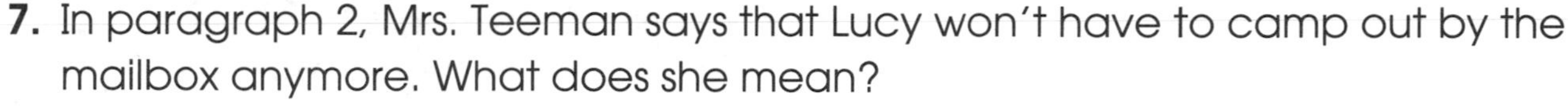

______ Lucy twirled around with a bunch of bananas for a partner.

______ Mrs. Teeman laughed at Lucy's excitement.

7. In paragraph 2, Mrs. Teeman says that Lucy won't have to camp out by the mailbox anymore. What does she mean?

____

____

Phone Troubles

What happens when Kyle doesn't pay attention to a telephone message?

1 Somebody called for Mom. It was somebody from school. I didn't really catch the name. I said my mom was mowing the lawn, and so the lady asked if I could take a message. I said, "Sure."

2 Then, she started talking about cakes and Thursday after school and I said sure, cakes were great. I was trying to get my math homework done because Raj was waiting for me next door. Then, the lady said something about the principal and I said, "Sure, I know," because everyone knows the principal. Finally, she stopped talking and said, "Okay?"

3 I said, "Okay." Then, I remembered to say, "Thank you for calling," just like Mom taught me. Then, I hung up, finished my math, and headed for Raj's house.

4 I didn't remember the call until the next morning at breakfast. "Oh, you had a call yesterday while you were out mowing the lawn, Mom."

5 "Oh? Who was it, Kyle?" she said, between toast bites.

6 *Uhhh. Think, think.* "It was about Thursday after school," I said, announcing the only detail I could remember.

7 "What about it?" Mom was getting a little prickly. I knew I had to handle this well.

8 "There's a bake sale. The principal was asking for stuff." I felt good about remembering the principal.

9 Well, to make a long story short, it was the president of the PTO who called. Mom said she's very important. She was asking if Mom could bake a cake for the principal because they were going to surprise him for his birthday.

10 Mom showed up on Thursday after school with a little plate of cookies, thinking there was a bake sale. Mrs. Essman looked at her like she was from Mars and asked where the cake was. Of course, Mom didn't know anything about a cake or a birthday or anything. Now, I'm in the doghouse, and my brother and I have to learn telephone manners from Mom.

NAME ______________________________

1. Number the sentences to show the order in which things happened.
   ______ Kyle gives Mom the phone message.
   ______ Mom goes to school on Thursday.
   ______ Mom goes out to mow the lawn.
   ______ Kyle takes a phone call for Mom.
   ______ Mrs. Essman asks Mom where the cake is.

2. Why does Mom take cookies to school on Thursday?

   ____

   ____

3. While he is talking on the phone, Kyle is also ______________________________

   ____.

4. What is the setting for this story?

   ____

   ____

5. What type of story is this?
   ______ realistic fiction ______ science fiction ______ a tall tale

6. In paragraph 7, the author says that Mom is getting a little prickly. What does this mean?

   ____

   ____

7. What do you think Kyle will do the next time he answers the phone? Why?

   ____

   ____

8. Do you think it was fair for Kyle's mom to be frustrated with him? Explain.

   ____

   ____

   ____

Phone Manners

What telephone manners does Mom teach her sons?

1 "Now, repeat after me. When we answer the phone, we say: 'Hello. Reese residence. This is so-and-so speaking.'"

2 My brother and I repeated after Mom in slow, droning tones, "Hello. Reese residence. This is Kyle-thony speaking." We each said our names in the "so-and-so" spot, so Kyle and Anthony came out *Kyle-thony*. I thought about giggling, but the look on Mom's face told me not to.

3 "That's very good." Mom was talking to us as if we were four-year-olds. "Now," she continued, "if the person on the other end of the phone says, 'May I speak to your mother?', what do you say? Kyle?" I knew this one.

4 I recited just like Mom had taught us. "Yes, you may. May I ask who is calling, please?"

5 "That's very good," said Mom in her sing-songy teacher voice. "Okay, you seem to have the basics. Let's talk about taking phone messages." She shot me a look. I had goofed up on one little phone message the other day. That's why my brother and I were in the Phone Manners from Mom class. "What are the three basic parts of a phone message?"

6 Anthony and I recited: "Name. Number. Write it down."

7 "Very good," sang Mom. "Oh, and there's actually a fourth part. Can anyone figure out what it is?" She looked right at me. I couldn't think.

8 "Deliver the message," Mom answered her own question, "on the same day the call comes in." I smiled weakly. That was a small detail that I had overlooked the other day, along with name, number, and writing it down.

9 "Any questions?" Mom asked brightly. Anthony raised his hand. "Yes?"

10 "Will there be a test?"

11 "Every time the phone rings," said Mom, quite seriously. "Class dismissed."

NAME ______________________

1. What important parts of a phone message did Kyle forget the other day?

____

____

2. Look at the illustration. What do you think Mom is saying? Write the dialogue.

____

____

3. Why is Mom talking to the boys as though they are four years old?

____

____

4. Look at the picture of Kyle and Anthony. What do you learn about the boys from the picture that isn't in the story?

____

____

5. How will the boys be tested?

____

____

6. Do you think Mom's phone class will be a success? Why or why not?

____

____

You have just attended the Phone Manners from Mom class. How should you respond to these telephone situations?

7. The phone rings. You answer it by saying, "______________________

______________________."

8. Your dad is reading a book on the porch. The phone rings and the person says, "May I speak to your father?" What do you say?

____

9. Your mom is washing her hair and can't come to the phone, so you must take a message. What are the four important parts of a phone message?

____

Hold the Phone!

What do the boys notice about Uncle Dale?

1 Kyle hung up the phone and tore the top sheet off the message pad. He posted it in the middle of the refrigerator door with his favorite magnet. Ever since Mom's Phone Manners class, he had followed the rules: Get the name. Get the number. Write it down. Deliver it.

2 As Kyle positioned the polar bear magnet, his uncle Dale walked into the kitchen. "Hey, Uncle Dale. What's up?"

3 "Oh, not much," shrugged Uncle Dale. "Your mom invited me over for supper." Uncle Dale often dropped by just in time for a meal.

4 "Oh, cool," said Kyle, on his way out the door with Anthony. Just then, the phone rang. Uncle Dale answered it.

5 "Yeah?" he said. Kyle and Anthony froze. Their mom had taught them not to say "yeah" on the phone. She said it was bad manners. They wondered how Uncle Dale had missed that lesson. "Yeah." Uncle Dale said again and nodded. "Yeah, okay." Silence. "Sure." He hung up.

6 After a moment, Anthony was too curious not to ask. "Who was that?"

7 "It was for your mom," said Uncle Dale, paging through a magazine. Kyle and Anthony looked at each other.

8 "Um, there's a message pad here," offered Kyle, "if you want to write a message down."

9 Uncle Dale looked up for a moment. "Oh, it's okay. I'll remember. It was someone from school about a meeting."

10 "What meeting?" asked Mom, peeling off her garden gloves at the kitchen door. Uncle Dale looked up.

11 "Oh, hi, Sis. Ahh, there's a meeting ... on Saturday morning." Uncle Dale's face suddenly looked a little pained.

12 "Where? What about?" asked Mom. Kyle and Anthony gritted their teeth.

13 "Oh, you know, one of those school meetings," said Uncle Dale slowly. "It starts at 9:30...I think."

14 Mom made a face. She looked at her sons. All three of them turned to Uncle Dale and recited: "Get the name! Get the number! Write it down! Deliver it!"

NAME ______________________________

1. What surprised Kyle and Anthony about Uncle Dale's phone conversation?

   ______ the fact that he had even answered the phone

   ______ the way he spoke

   ______ the length of the conversation

2. Number the sentences to show the order in which events happened.

   ______ Uncle Dale gets a lesson on how to take phone messages.

   ______ Uncle Dale arrives.

   ______ Uncle Dale answers the phone.

   ______ Kyle takes a phone message.

   ______ Mom enters the kitchen.

   ______ Kyle greets Uncle Dale.

3. Why does Uncle Dale's face look a little pained in paragraph 11?

   ____

   ____

4. Why are Kyle and Anthony not supposed to say "yeah" on the phone?

   ____

   ____

5. How are Uncle Dale and Mom related to each other?

   ____

   ____

6. Do you think that Uncle Dale will use better phone manners in the future? Explain.

   ____

   ____

   ____

Telephones: How Do They Work?

Read to find out how telephones work.

1 We're going to take a little trip. We're going to travel with your voice as it leaves your mouth, goes through a telephone, moves through the telephone network, and arrives at your friend's telephone.

2 Let's say you already dialed the telephone. A computer instantly connected you to your friend's telephone, based on the numbers you pressed. The sound waves made by your voice enter the microphone in your telephone. The sound waves then travel by wire. With the help of an electric power supply, an electric current runs along the wire. Your sound waves disrupt that flow of electricity. When the current is flowing smoothly, your friend hears no sound. When your sound waves have affected the flow, the varying electrical current reaches the speaker in the earpiece of your friend's telephone. A device there changes the electrical currents back into sound waves. The sound waves enter your friend's ear, and your conversation has begun.

3 As technology goes, telephones are thought to be quite simple. People knew almost 400 years ago that sound waves could travel along a wire. Then, in 1875, Alexander Graham Bell invented a telephone that could be put to practical use. Imagine what he would think if he could see his fellow Americans on the telephone today.

NAME ______________________

1. The article says it's not your voice, but ______________ made by your voice, that enter the telephone's microphone.

2. When the current in a telephone wire is flowing smoothly, what does the person on the other end hear?

____

3. When sound waves interrupt the flow of current, what does the person on the other end hear?

____

4. How long ago did people know that sound could travel along a wire?

____

5. How long ago did Alexander Graham Bell invent the telephone?

____

Write **F** next to each sentence that is a fact. Write **O** next to each sentence that is an opinion.

6. ______ Sound waves travel along a wire with the help of an electrical current.

7. ______ The telephone is the most important invention of the last 200 years.

8. ______ Without the telephone, modern businesses would fail.

9. How does the computer know to connect you to the person you are trying to call?

____

10. **Telephones have been around for less than a hundred years.** Is this statement true or false?

____

11. How do you and other members of your family use the telephone today?

____

____

12. What would it be like if you had to get along without telephones? How else would you communicate?

____

____

Honey to the Rescue

What happens when there is no syrup for the pancakes?

1 *What's that smell?* I snuggled under the covers. I was still too close to sleep to identify it. It was a good smell, but it wasn't a normal smell. *What day is it? Saturday? What's that smell?*

2 My brain finally jerked me awake as I began to put the pieces together. Saturday. That smell...pancakes! I grabbed my fuzzy robe and rushed down the stairs. Mom stood at the griddle, humming and flipping pancakes. Without a word, I slid into my spot.

3 Dad nodded at me. He was spooning mushed up baby food from a jar into my little brother's mouth. Poor kid. He was too young to eat pancakes. My little sister sat at the table, fork in hand, quiet for once, waiting for her pancakes.

4 Mom turned away from the griddle with the first plateful of pancakes. I smiled charmingly at her; she smiled back. Two for Dad, two for Lisa, two for me. *Excellent.* I spread some butter, then reached for the syrup. *Nope, no syrup.* I went to the refrigerator and opened the door. I looked in the usual spots. I looked again: on the door shelves, behind the milk jug, behind the orange juice. Panic rose. I turned and scanned the kitchen counter. *Nope, no syrup.*

5 "Mom?" I asked calmly. "Where's the syrup?"

6 She kept flipping. "Isn't it there in the door? Or behind the milk?"

7 "No. I looked twice." But I looked again, just to make sure. Then, Mom looked.

8 "Oh, don't tell me we're out. I was sure we had some," she moaned.

9 Dad paused his spooning. "I can run to the store, I guess."

10 "Oh, wait," interrupted Mom. She stepped up onto a stool and reached up to the top shelf in the cupboard. Out came a plastic bear. "Honey to the rescue!" she announced. "Gramps sent this last summer. I keep forgetting about it."

11 She plunked the bear down on the table and went back to the griddle. *Well, there's no syrup, so there's no choice.* I swirled some of the bear's golden goop onto my pancakes. I tasted. I chewed. I smiled. *Honey to the rescue, indeed.*

NAME ____________________

1. What clues tell you that the narrator is in bed? Write the words or phrases from the story.

____

____

2. How do you know that having pancakes for breakfast must be a special thing?

____

____

3. The word that best describes this family is
   ______ rough.
   ______ noisy.
   ______ pleasant.

4. What is the setting for this story?

____

____

5. Write two things you know about the narrator of the story.

____

____

6. Why does the girl feel sorry for her younger brother?

____

____

7. Explain the title of the story, "Honey to the Rescue."

____

____

8. Why is the first sentence of the story ("*What's that smell?*") in italics?

____

____

Honey

What are the author's opinions about honey?

1 Honey lasts pretty much forever. That's one reason why it should be our national food. Did you know they found honey in one of the pyramids? It wasn't moldy or rotten. They tasted it, and it still tasted like honey. It didn't taste like 3,000-year-old honey; it just tasted like honey. Those Egyptian bees must have been something else.

2 Honey is sweet. That's another reason it should be our national food. Americans love sweet things. I happen to like sweet things, and honey is at the top of my list. I use honey to sweeten my tea and my breakfast cereal. I put it on bread and toast. I use it instead of part of the sugar when I bake certain cookies and breads. Have you had a honey-glazed ham lately? Yum!

3 I think the bees would like it if we made honey our national food. People would plant special gardens. The bees could gather nectar everywhere. Nectar is sort of like sugar water. Flowers produce it to attract bees and butterflies. While gathering nectar, the creatures just happen to get pollen on them, which they take to the next flower. The flowers would not survive without this mixing of pollen. Then, bees mix a special substance called an *enzyme* with the nectar. To avoid a long explanation, let's just say it changes the nectar into a special kind of sugar that we call *honey*.

4 Bees don't just make honey; they eat it, too. Or, rather, they feed it to young bees, called *larvae*, in the hive. Honey also is used to keep the bees' food from spoiling. Bees store pollen in cells within the hive. Each cell is then sealed with honey to prevent bacteria from entering.

5 See how useful honey is? Even if it's not our national food, stop and admire a honey bee some day, and remember to say thank you. Then, go have some bread and honey.

NAME ______________________

1. List the reasons the author gives for making honey our national food.

____

____

2. Do you think those are good reasons for naming honey as a national food? Write why or why not.

____

____

3. Sometimes, an author has more than one purpose for writing. What two purposes do you think this author had for writing the honey article?

   ______ to entertain readers
   ______ to give an explanation of honey bees' lives
   ______ to persuade readers that honey is good
   ______ to describe how honey resists bacteria

4. This article is mostly about

   ______ how good honey is.
   ______ the food value of honey.

Write the best word to complete each sentence below.

5. It's amazing that the honey didn't ______________. (burst, spoil, mend)

6. I like to ______________ honey on hot toast. (spread, clap, handle)

7. As bees ______________ nectar, they also spread pollen. (collect, enter, change)

8. What would happen to flowers without bees and butterflies?

____

9. This article contains facts about bees and honey, but it also contains the author's opinion. Give one example of each.

   Fact: ______________________________________

   Opinion: ___________________________________

10. Name one way in which bees use the honey they make.

____

A Sad Song

Read to see why people sing songs.

1 *"....Then mend it, dear Georgie, dear Georgie, dear Georgie. Then mend it, dear Georgie. Dear Georgie, mend it."*

2 Eliza raised her hand. Mr. Hamlin, the music teacher, had been watching her. She hadn't been singing. "Eliza?"

3 Eliza looked puzzled. "I understand why people would want to make a song about someone named Liza...." Eliza began. Several classmates turned around and made good-natured faces at her. "But why would anyone want to make a song about a dumb bucket with a hole in it?" A burst of giggling came from the class.

4 "Hmm, well that's a good question," answered Mr. Hamlin. "Would anyone like to guess?"

5 "You told us it was an old song, so I suppose people would have used buckets a lot," Natalie offered.

6 "That's right," encouraged Mr. Hamlin. "A bucket would have been a very common thing." Mr. Hamlin let them think some more. Then, he went on. "Remember last week when we worked on 'Down by the Well'? What did we say about that song?"

7 Jansen remembered. "We said that going to the well to get water was something people did every day."

8 "So," cut in Eliza,"they made up songs about stuff they did every day?"

9 Mr. Hamlin gave a big nod. "People sang songs when they were happy or sad, when they worked, or when they rested. Songs helped people express their feelings."

10 "I guess that's not much different from us," said Eliza, still thinking it over. "I sang a sad song just this morning."

11 "Oh? What about?" said Mr. Hamlin.

12 Eliza sang her answer. *"There's a hole in my sock, dear Mommy, dear Mommy...."*

NAME ______________________________

1. Write **R** next to two sentences that tell about real things.

    ______ Anyone can make up a song.

    ______ A song can be happy or sad.

    ______ The words of a song are always true.

2. Read the sentences below. Write **F** next to sentences that are facts and **O** next to sentences that are opinions.

    ______ Eliza raised her hand.

    ______ Well, that's a good question.

    ______ I guess that's not much different from us.

    ______ Mr. Hamlin let them think some more.

3. Choose one piece of dialogue from the story, and write it on the line. Tell what the dialogue tells you about the character or the story.

    ____

    ____

    ____

4. The students figure out that people like to make up songs about ______________

    ____.

5. Earlier that day, Eliza says she sang a song about her ______________.

6. Which word best describes Eliza?

    ______ curious

    ______ sneaky

    ______ nervous

7. If you wrote a song, what everyday things could you put in it?

    ____

    ____

    ____

What Is Folk Music?

Do you know any folk songs?

1 Wouldn't you like to know how people used to live, what they did, and how they felt about things? Sing a folk song, and maybe you'll find out!

2 Though people still write folk music, most of the songs we think of as folk songs are old. They come from America's earliest settlements, from war battlefields, and from pioneers' log cabins. And, of course, some of the songs' roots go even farther back to the settlers' original countries.

3 We don't know who wrote most folk music. What we do know we learn from the words of the songs. They tell about everyday life, soldiers lost in wars, and hard work. The words tell us that people's feelings haven't changed much over the last few hundred years.

4 Within the body of folk music are two types of songs. Ballads are longer songs that usually relate a story. They may be serious or funny. Folk songs are shorter songs that might relate a feeling or an experience a person had.

5 Folk music covers endless topics and countless emotions. Coming up with an average folk song or ballad is almost impossible because there is so much variety. Here, however, is the first verse of "Farewell, Nancy." In it, a sailor expresses both sadness and hope. These feelings are common to many folk songs.

Farewell, my dearest Nancy,
Since I must now leave you;
Unto the salt seas
I am bound for to go;
But let my long absence
Be no trouble to you,
For I shall return
In the spring, as you know.

NAME ______________________________

1. What is the difference between a ballad and a folk song?

____

____

2. Why do you suppose someone wrote "Farewell, Nancy"?

____

____

3. Why do you think someone would make a song about saying good-bye?

____

____

4. "When Johnny Comes Marching Home Again" is a well-known ballad. Even if you don't know the words, the title hints at the song's story. What do you think it is?

____

____

5. Write **T** for **true** or **F** for **false** next to each statement below.

   ______ People's feelings are very different today than they were long ago.

   ______ Most folk songs have been written recently.

   ______ Folk music can be about a number of different topics and emotions.

6. Why do you think people might write folk songs during wars?

____

____

7. What two main emotions does the sailor have in "Farewell Nancy"?

   ______________ and ______________

8. Why do you think that we don't know who wrote most folk songs?

____

____

Peanut Butter Plus

Read to see what the boys learn about their grandpa.

1 "Thicker, please," requested Max. His grandmother looked at him with a raised eyebrow.

2 Max shrugged. "I really like it."

3 "All right," sighed Grandma, "a little more, but then that's enough, I think."

4 "Thanks, Grandma," smiled Max. Grandma, Max, and A.J. were putting together a picnic. They were going to take it to the far field to check on Grandpa, who was planting corn.

5 "May I have one just like that?" asked A.J. "Please?" Grandma just laughed and shook her head.

6 "I never have seen anyone who likes peanut butter as much as you two do," she said, shaking her head.

7 The boys grinned. It was true. They loved peanut butter. A peanut butter and jelly sandwich for lunch every day made them perfectly happy.

8 Grandma went on. "Of course, it was your grandpa who invented the best peanut butter sandwich ever."

9 The boys had never heard this story. They threw questions at her. "How? When? What is it?"

10 Grandma looked out the window, as if the story were out there. "It was when we were first married. Your grandpa had broken his leg and couldn't do any farm work. So I was out on the tractor. The hay had to be brought in, after all. Grandpa had never really cooked, but he felt as if he should have a meal ready when I came in from the field. So he put together a peanut butter-bacon-banana sandwich on toast. I thought it looked awful, but I didn't want to hurt his feelings. So I took a bite." Grandma stopped, daydreaming out the window.

11 The boys couldn't wait. "And?"

12 A little smile curved at Grandma's lips. "It was delicious."

NAME ______________________________

1. What do Grandma and Grandpa do for a living?

____

____

2. Do you think Grandma likes peanut butter? Why?

____

____

3. Do you think you would like a peanut butter-bacon-banana sandwich?

____

____

4. What do you think will happen next?

____

____

5. Write **C** next to the sentence below that is the cause. Write **E** next to the sentence that is the effect.

______ Grandma helped out in the fields.

______ Grandpa broke his leg.

6. Where are Max and A.J. taking their picnic?

____

____

7. What would Max and A.J. like to have for lunch better than anything else?

____

____

8. Why did Grandma eat the sandwich, even though it sounded awful to her?

____

____

Working for Peanuts

Who is responsible for the popularity of peanuts?

1 What can you do with nuts? A scientist named George Washington Carver answered that question, over and over again. We owe thanks to him for more than 300 products.

2 When Carver was born in 1864, he was a slave on a farm in Missouri. Later, as a teenager and a freedman, he worked on a farm and managed to put himself through high school. At age 30, he became the first black student at his college in Iowa. In 1896, he became the first black teacher to be hired at another college in Iowa. Several years later, he took a job at a college in Alabama, where he worked until his death in 1943.

3 Carver studied agriculture, the science of farming. His research made huge improvements in farming in the southern United States. In particular, Carver studied peanuts. He knew that the South could not grow only cotton. Planting cotton year after year wore out the soil and made it useless. Carver learned that if farmers planted cotton one year and peanuts the next, the soil remained healthy.

4 To encourage this practice, Carver came up with new uses for the peanut. Would you like to try peanut and prune ice cream? How about lotion or shampoo made from peanuts? Perhaps you would prefer to make paint from peanuts, or maybe you would like to bake with peanut flour. Glue? Paper? Rubber? The list goes on and on. He also came up with similar uses for pecans and other nuts.

5 Carver did not profit from most of his inventions. He didn't feel that it was right to sell his ideas. Rather, he gave them freely to help farmers and fellow scientists. Carver's life is one that we could all use as an example.

NAME ______________________________

1. This article is mostly about
   ______ Carver's work with peanuts.
   ______ Carver's fame as a scientist.
   ______ Carver's fight to get an education.
2. George Washington Carver lived from __________ until __________.
3. While in college, he studied ______________________________, which is the study of ______________________________.
4. Carver made hundreds of products from peanuts. List some that the article mentions.

   ____

5. Which of the products seems the most interesting or the most unusual to you? Write why.

   ____

   ____

Write **F** next to each sentence that is a fact. Write **O** next to each sentence that is an opinion.

6. ______ Carver saved Southern farmers from ruining the land.
7. ______ Planting peanuts after cotton keeps the soil healthy.
8. ______ Carver is America's greatest black scientist.
9. Based on the article, it seems that the author __________ Carver.
   ______ dislikes
   ______ admires
   ______ ignores
10. Why is it a good idea to rotate crops, instead of planting the same thing over and over?

    ____

    ____

11. Reread the first line of paragraph 5. Do you feel that Carver made the right choices? Explain.

    ____

    ____

All Wrapped Up

What kind of wrapping paper do Stephanie and her mom use?

1 "Do you really think he'll like it?" I asked Mom for the fiftieth time. She gave me the same answer every time.

2 "Of course he will, Steph, and mostly because you made it."

3 I wasn't completely sure about her answer. I wanted him to like his Father's Day present because it was great, not just because I made it. Dad had been talking about building a birdhouse all winter. He just hadn't had time. So, I asked Mom to help me make one. One wall was a little crooked, but other than that it looked pretty good, I thought.

4 We had nailed the roof on after school. Now, we were hunting in the attic for a box to put the birdhouse in.

5 "Is this one big enough?" I asked, holding up an old shoe box.

6 "Mmm, I don't think the roof would quite fit. Here's one. What do you think?" asked Mom.

7 "Looks good. I'm sure that'll be big enough. Let's go wrap it." Father's Day was two days away, but I was eager to have my present all ready.

8 "Okay. I have a great idea for wrapping paper," said Mom. She loved to drop hints.

9 "Oh, did you buy some new stuff?" I asked.

10 "Nope," said Mom simply.

11 "Uhhh, well, what's the idea, then?" You just never knew with my mom.

12 Mom spread out a big sheet of plain light brown paper. There were already some paints sitting on the counter, along with some sponges and rubber stamps. Mom waved her arms over the collection. "We're going to print our own wrapping paper. Won't that make your present extra special?"

13 Well, I thought my present was already extra special, but if it made Mom happy, I guess I would do it. "Okay. Extra special paper for an extra special present. Let's do it."

NAME ______________________

Write the best word to complete each sentence below.

1. Stephanie and her mom look for a box in the ______________.
(attic, entrance, ending)

2. Stephanie was proud that she had ______________ her present.
(waved, built, filled)

3. Stephanie was ______________ about Mom's wrapping idea.
(clever, crazy, curious)

4. Explain how Stephanie will make the wrapping paper.

____

____

____

5. Write two adjectives you could use to describe Stephanie.

______________ and ______________

6. Look at the picture. Where do you think Stephanie and her mom are?
______ in the living room ______ in the garage ______ in Stephanie's room

7. From whose point of view is the story told?

____

____

8. Do you think Dad will like Stephanie's gift? Why or why not?

____

____

____

Making Prints

Read to see how to create your own prints.

1 Making prints is easy and fun, and there is no limit to the designs you can make.

Supplies

paints (tempera or acrylic)

paintbrushes

stamps* (see note below)

sheets of tissue or craft paper

plastic lids

newspaper

* Use store-bought rubber or sponge stamps. Or make your own stamps, using household materials such as fruits or vegetables, kitchen utensils, bottle caps, office supplies, and so on.

Instructions

1. Cover your work area with newspaper.
2. Pour small amounts of paint into plastic lids (so you can easily dip your stamps into the paint).
3. Lay out a sheet of paper. Imagine the design you are going to print.
4. Dip a stamp into some paint. If you want to use more than one color for a stamp, apply paint to areas of the stamp with a paintbrush.
5. Press the stamp, paint side down, firmly on the paper without jiggling or sliding the stamp from side to side.
6. Hold the paper down with one hand while you lift the stamp.
7. Repeat steps 4, 5, and 6 until your design is complete.
8. Let paper dry. To clean up, wash stamps and paintbrushes in warm, soapy water.

2 In addition to making wrapping paper, you can use this same process to decorate boxes, book covers, or even walls and furniture (with permission, of course). Use your imagination and print away!

NAME ______________________________

1. The author used a numbered list for the instructions. Why do you think this was done?

____

____

2. What other kinds of instructions, with numbered lists, have you seen?

____

3. Number the sentences to show the order in which to complete the stamping project.

______ Dip stamp into paint.
______ Press stamp on paper.
______ Put paint in plastic lids.
______ Let dry.
______ Lay out sheet of paper.
______ Lift the stamp.

4. Why do the instructions say you should put small amounts of paint in plastic lids?

____

____

5. What can you think of that you would like to decorate with stamps?

____

____

6. Explain how you can make your own stamps.

____

____

7. What is the author's purpose?

______ to instruct ______ to entertain ______ to persuade

8. Does this sound like a craft you would like to try? Why or why not?

____

____

____

Answer Key

1. This story is mostly about
   ______ a sleepover.
   ______ Sam's parents.
   __X__ two boys' plans.
2. At the beginning, when Sam and Kent are talking on the phone, what did you think they might be talking about?
   Answers will vary.
3. In the story, when did you find out what the boys are planning?
   when Sam asks his parents for permission
4. Why do you think Sam told his dad about the grass clippings?
   Answers will vary.
5. Why does Sam mention being warm enough and when the lights will be turned out?
   Answers will vary.
6. Now that the boys have permission, what do you think they will do next?
   Answers will vary.
7. In paragraph 5, why are the words *Now, if we can only talk our parents into letting us do this* in italics?
   Sam is not speaking out loud. He is thinking those words.
8. What is the author's purpose in writing this selection?
   to entertain
9. Have you ever been worried about asking your parents to do something? What was it, and how did you ask them?
   Answers will vary.

3

1. One of the boys usually has the ideas. The other one seems to go along with those ideas. Which boy is the "leader"?
   Sam
2. What details from the story helped you answer question 1?
   Answers will vary.
3. Kent says he might help his mom with supper. What does that tell you about Kent?
   Answers will vary.
4. Based on what you know about camping, how do you feel about all the stuff the boys have in their tent? List what you think they need and what they don't need.
   What They Need
   Answers will vary.
   What They Don't Need
   Answers will vary.
5. In some stories, the author tells you what is happening. In this story, the author uses mostly dialogue, what the characters say, to let you know what is going on. Choose one line of dialogue and write what it helps you know about the character.
   Dialogue: Ex.: "Oh, no! We're camping. Those are just for in the house..."
   Answers will vary.
6. Why does Kent think that Sam knows more about camping?
   Possible answer: The tent belongs to Sam's dad, so Kent figures Sam knows something about camping.
7. How do you think the boys feel about camping out together? Explain your answer.
   Answers will vary.

5

1. What do you know about pitching a tent? Do you have anything to add to these instructions?
   Answers will vary.
2. Number the sentences to show the order of steps to pitch a tent.
   __3__ Spread out groundcloth.
   __7__ Tighten and peg guy lines.
   __1__ Choose and clear an area.
   __5__ Put together tent poles.
   __2__ Lay out equipment.
   __4__ Pound stakes through loops.
   __6__ Raise the poles.
3. If you don't know or understand what a guy line is, which illustration helps you figure it out? Tell how.
   The illustration that goes with Step 7; the guy lines are stretched out, just as the text describes.
4. Choose one illustration. Explain what it shows.
   Answers will vary.
5. In the first paragraph, the author says that pitching a tent alone is difficult. Why do you think this is?
   Possible answer: It is hard to put in the poles and raise the tent alone.
6. What is the purpose of a groundcloth?
   Possible answer: to protect the bottom of the tent
7. Which two steps explain what to do with the poles?
   5 and 6
8. After reading these instructions, do you think you could pitch a tent? Why or why not?
   Answers will vary.

7

1. Which sentence best describes this story?
   __X__ Nothing exciting happens to the boys in the tent.
   ______ The boys have a crazy night in the tent.
   ______ In the morning, Kent plays a trick on Sam and scares him.
2. Why did the boys stop playing badminton?
   Sam finds crumbs in his sleeping bag.
3. Read the sentences below. Write **F** next to sentences that are facts and **O** next to sentences that are opinions.
   __O__ Kent eats too many crackers.
   __F__ Sam's dad had been telling camping stories for almost an hour.
   __F__ Breakfast is ready.
   __O__ Sam's dad tells the best camping stories.
4. What do you think the boys were hoping would happen?
   Answers will vary.
5. In paragraph 3, why does Kent turn red?
   Answers will vary. Possible answer: He was surprised.
6. Write **C** next to the sentence below that is the cause. Write **E** next to the sentence that is the effect.
   __E__ Kent landed on top of Sam.
   __C__ Sam's mom startled the boys.
7. This story has two settings. What are they?
   Sam's kitchen and the tent

9

Answer Key

1. What is causing Mikki to worry?
   She sees lights flashing outside.
2. What does Mikki do to try to get to sleep?
   First, she turns away from the window and closes her eyes
   Then, she rolls toward the window and tries to figure out what it is
3. What is causing the flashing lights?
   There is a thunderstorm far in the distance. Mikki is seeing only the lightning.
4. Have you ever been kept awake at night by something that bothered or puzzled you? Write about it.
   Answers will vary.
5. From whose point of view is this story told?
   ___ Mom's X Mikki's ___ Uncle Walt's
6. Which word best describes Mom in the story?
   ___ impatient ___ confused X kind
7. Is this story realistic? Why or why not?
   yes; Possible answer: The things that happen in the story could happen in real life.
8. Name three things that Mikki thinks the lights could be. **Possible answers:**
   car lights police car flashers space ships

11

1. The author wrote this article to
   ___ entertain.
   X give information.
   ___ persuade.
2. Which comes first, thunder or lightning?
   Lightning comes first.
3. What causes lightning? Give a brief answer.
   a build-up of electricity on water droplets
4. How does lightning cause thunder?
   Ex.: When lightning strikes, the air heats, then cools. The sudden changes in air temperature cause the sound.
5. If you read only the two headings in this article, what would you learn?
   Answers will vary.
6. Write **T** for true or **F** for false next to each statement below.
   F Thunder always takes the same amount of time to reach Earth.
   T Light travels faster than sound.
   F Thunder and lightning are not related to each other.
7. What is the main idea of paragraph 4?
   Possible answer: Lightning happens when the electrical charge in droplets has to discharge.
8. Which of the following is the purpose of paragraph 1?
   X introduction ___ author's purpose ___ conclusion

13

Put a check next to the sentences that are true.

1. ✓ The idea for Smokey the Bear started in the 1940s.
2. ___ Smokey the Bear lives in New Mexico.
3. ___ The Forest Service made posters in honor of a bear cub that died in a fire.
4. ✓ Smokey the Bear was a drawing first, and then a real bear.

Write **M** next to the sentences that tell about make-believe things.

5. ___ Smokey the Bear lived in a zoo for many years.
6. M Smokey the Bear speaks to campers about the danger of forest fires.
7. M Smokey the Bear used to help firefighters put out fires.
8. Why was Smokey the Bear created? Write the phrase or sentence from the article that tells you.
   to protect America's forests
9. In paragraph 2, what problem did U.S. leaders have?
   They were worried about having enough wood for the war.
10. What was the solution?
    to start a campaign to prevent forest fires
11. What organization created the fire safety posters?
    the Forest Service
12. In the posters, did Smokey the Bear look realistic? Explain.
    Possible answer: No, he was wearing a park ranger's hat.

15

A **fact** is something that can be proven true. An **opinion** is what someone thinks or feels. Check the sentences that are facts.

1. ✓ Vegetables can be grown in pots.
2. ___ Creating a garden on a fire escape is difficult.
3. ___ Any garden is beautiful.
4. ✓ Plants need soil and water.
5. Number the sentences to show the order in which things happened.
   3 Rosa bought potting soil.
   2 Rosa took the pots home.
   4 Rosa planted her seeds.
   1 Rosa saw the pots.
6. Check the words or phrases that best describe Rosa.
   ___ selfish
   ___ tends to waste time
   ✓ likes the outdoors
   ✓ appreciates beauty
7. Why do you think Rosa slept well the night after she bought seeds and soil?
   Possible answer: She felt happy and content.
8. The author repeats a line from paragraph 4 in the last paragraph. What line is it? Why do you think the author repeats it?
   "masses of flowers and fat, glowing fruits." Possible answer: It's something Rosa likes to repeat to herself to remind her of what her garden will be like.
9. Have you ever planted something and watched it grow? Tell about how it made you feel.
   Answers will vary.

17

Answer Key

1. Why is Rosa worried about her plants on this day?
   She is afraid the heat and lack of rain will hurt her plants.

Write T if the sentence is true. Write F if the sentence is false.

2. F This story is mostly about Rosa worrying about her garden.
3. F Rosa is careless about her garden.
4. T Rosa plans to share her flowers with others.
5. T Too much sun causes Rosa's plants to dry up.

Compare how things really are with how they used to be, or with what Rosa imagines.

6. The strongest, tallest tomato plant is pale and dry looking.
   It had been green and smooth.
7. Rosa bites into an apple.
   She imagines that it is a big, juicy tomato.
8. She chops a carrot.
   She imagines that it is a shiny green pepper.
9. For now, Rosa works at a factory.
   She dreams of running her own flower shop.
10. Why do you think Rosa spends so much time daydreaming?
    Possible answer: She doesn't like her job, and her life is not very colorful or interesting.
11. What details from the story helped you answer question 10?
    Answers will vary.
12. Which of these is mostly likely to be true?
    ___ Rosa lives in the country.
    ✓ Rosa lives in a city.

19

1. What do you know about peppers, or what experiences have you had growing or eating peppers?
   Answers will vary.
2. Do you like peppers? Write why or why not.
   Answers will vary.
3. How are bell peppers and chili peppers the same? How are they different? Write what the article tells you about each kind.

   Bell Peppers
   Size apple-sized
   Shape round
   Color red, yellow, or green
   Flavor less spicy

   Chili Peppers
   Size many sizes
   Shape long and skinny
   Color red, yellow, or green
   Flavor hot or spicy
4. What two headings does the author divide the article into? How is this helpful?
   Bell Peppers and Chili Peppers; Possible answer: The sections help you know where to look for information in the article.
5. Write T for true or F for false next to each statement below.
   T Hot peppers can make your eyes water.
   F Bell peppers are very spicy.
   T Peppers can be prepared in many ways.
   F Bell peppers are red, and chili peppers are green.
6. What makes chili peppers burn your mouth?
   a chemical in them
7. What two vitamins are peppers high in?
   A and C

21

1. What was Joseph's main goal in getting a job at 17?
   to help support his family
2. Why did Joseph always make a point to walk past the bakery?
   He loved the way it smelled.
3. Who started work earlier, Joseph or the pie bakers?
   the pie bakers
4. Who is the main character in this story?
   Joseph Fellini
5. Would you describe young Joseph as serious or dreamy? Write why.
   Answers will vary.
6. How did Joseph feel about his job?
   He had enjoyed it. It made him feel important.
7. Do you think Joseph was a good worker? Explain.
   Answers will vary.
8. Do you think Joseph has lived in the same city his whole life? Explain.
   Possible answer: Yes. He walked past the bakery in high school. As an old man, he still lives in the same area.
9. At the end of the story, how does Joseph feel when he sees a young pie man act impatiently?
   Possible answer: He thinks the young man should slow down—he is just at the beginning of his career.

23

1. As you began to read about Mr. Fellini's walk in the park, what did you think was going to happen?
   Answers will vary.
2. Predict what Mr. Fellini will do next.
   Answers will vary.
3. Which of these does Mr. Fellini see on his walk?
   ___ a work of art
   X children and turtles
   X mothers and baby strollers
   ___ a nest of young birds
4. Which of these best describes Mr. Fellini?
   ✓ thoughtful ___ anxious ___ impatient
5. Reread the last two lines of paragraph 8. Why is it odd that the cars waited patiently?
   Possible answer: If there is a line of cars, I would expect the drivers to be impatient.
6. Why does Mr. Fellini think that the power-walking mothers should slow down?
   so that they can take the time to notice the birds and flowers
7. Write **C** next to the sentence below that is the cause. Write **E** next to the sentence that is the effect.
   C A line of mothers and baby strollers marched by.
   E Mr. Fellini had to step off the sidewalk.
8. Give an example of a line of dialogue from the story.
   Possible answer: "What'll it be today, Mr. Fellini?"
9. Mr. Fellini appreciates the small things in life. Do you agree or disagree? Why?
   Answers will vary.

25

Answer Key

1. The article contains a feature box titled "Central Park by the Numbers." What kind of information is in the box?
   The box gives information about the size of the park and the number of things in it.
2. Why do you think this information was shown in a separate list instead of in the text?
   Answers will vary.
3. When was Central Park planned?
   1858
4. The park was a daring project because
   the land was rocky, swampy, and muddy.
5. If you walked on all of the walking paths in the park, you would walk
   58 miles
6. Which is greater, the number of trees or the number of benches?
   the number of trees
7. For what reason was Central Park created?
   as a green space that gives people a break from the busy city
8. How is Central Park different from an average city park?
   It is much, much larger.
9. Have you ever visited Central Park? If you have, tell what it was like. If you haven't, tell what you might like to do there.
   Answers will vary.

27

1. In most stories, a character has a problem. What is Perry's problem?
   He feels awful during soccer practice.
2. What information in the story helped you answer question 1?
   Answers will vary.
3. **Dialogue** is what the characters in a story say. What did you learn about Perry from his dialogue?
   He doesn't ever want to go back to soccer practice.
4. Find a line of the coach's dialogue. What does it tell you about the coach?
   Dialogue: Answers will vary.
   What it tells: Answers will vary.
5. Coach thinks that a passing exercise is important because
   the players need to be able to pass the ball well during a game.
6. What is the setting for this story?
   the soccer field
7. **Practice was awful.** Is this a fact or an opinion?
   an opinion
8. The last line of paragraph 5 says that Perry didn't even wait for his mom's usual question. What do you think her question is?
   Possible answer: How was practice?
9. Which word or phrase best describes Perry in this story?
   _____ confident _____ full of energy __✓__ exhausted
10. Have you ever wished you could quit an activity? Tell about it.
    Answers will vary.

29

1. Mrs. Rothman is speechless because
   Perry has just said he wants to quit soccer.
2. Check two words that tell how Perry probably felt.
   __✓__ disappointed
   _____ proud
   _____ eager
   __✓__ frightened
3. Perry says he wants to quit soccer because
   he is weak; doesn't have what it takes.
4. Have you ever tried to do something that was hard, or that you had to work at? What was it?
   Answers will vary.
   Did you get discouraged? Did you quit?
   Answers will vary.
5. Do you think Perry's decision is reasonable, or do you think he is giving up too easily? Explain.
   Answers will vary.
6. Mrs. Rothman probably feels
   __✓__ surprised _____ angry _____ entertained
7. What problem does Mrs. Rothman think Perry is having?
   He didn't have a good lunch, so he was low on energy.
8. How does she plan to help Perry?
   She's going to make him a power snack to eat right before the next practice.
9. What do you think would be a good example of a power snack? Explain your choice.
   Answers will vary.

31

Write these steps in the correct order. (Not all of the recipe's steps are here.)
- spread mixture into pan
- drizzle glaze
- grease the pan
- mix sugar, oil, and eggs
- remove from oven and cool

1. grease the pan
2. mix sugar, oil, and eggs
3. spread mixture into pan
4. remove from oven and cool
5. drizzle glaze
6. How long do the directions say to bake the bars?
   16 to 22 minutes
7. The directions say to "drizzle honey glaze over bars." How did you know what honey glaze was?
   Answers will vary.

Recipes often use short forms of words called **abbreviations**. Match the common recipe words in the box with their abbreviations.

cup	teaspoon
Fahrenheit	tablespoon

8. T. tablespoon
10. F Fahrenheit
9. c. cup
11. tsp. teaspoon
12. The directions say, "Bake until center is set but not firm." What does this mean?
    Possible answer: The middle should not be gooey, but it should not be overbaked either.
13. How long do the energy bars need to cool?
    They need to cool completely.
14. What is the longest you could keep these bars? What would you need to do to them?
    six months; freeze them

33

Answer Key

1. When you read the story's title, did you guess about how the story ended? Was your guess close to being correct? Explain.
Answers will vary.

2. Circle the word that best describes the coach's words before the game.
angry (encouraging)

3. Have you ever been in a sporting event or a performance that didn't turn out the way you expected? Did something funny or weird happen? Write about it.
Answers will vary.

4. At the end of paragraph 2, Coach says that the players have "dribbled to the moon and back." This is a figure of speech. What does it mean?
Possible answer: They have dribbled a great distance.

5. Give one example of dialogue in the story.
Possible answer: "Okay, everybody listen up!"

Now, give one example of a character's thought that is not spoken out loud.
Possible answer: Now that was a solid kick.

6. How are the two examples in question 5 written differently from each other?
The first one is in quotation marks, and the second one is in italics.

7. Why is it funny that someone in the crowd says, "It's a home run!"?
Possible answer: There are no home runs in soccer. The person was confusing soccer with baseball.

35

1. This article is mostly about
____ how soccer was named.
____ the rules of soccer.
__✓__ soccer's history.

2. Historians think that soccer might have started out as a **skill-building exercise for soldiers**.

3. Why did King Edward III pass a law against soccer?
the game was rough or violent

4. What punishment did Queen Elizabeth have for soccer players?
a week of jail

5. What important rule change made the game into what we know as soccer? When did it happen?
In 1869 a rule against handling the ball with the hands was made.

6. If you wanted to find out about the beginnings of soccer, under which heading should you look?
Earliest Record

7. Under which heading would you find information about soccer during the last century or so?
The Modern Game Emerges

8. Write **T** for **true** or **F** for **false** next to each statement below.
__F__ Today, you are allowed to touch the ball with your hands in soccer.
__T__ Kicking and biting were common in soccer games long ago.
__T__ In Britain, soccer is called "football."

9. At the end of paragraph 3, it says, "the game could not be stopped." Why do you think this was true?
Possible answer: It was popular, and people loved it too much to stop playing.

10. What was the author's purpose for writing this article?
to tell about the history of soccer

37

1. The person who wrote this article is the **author**. The author probably wrote this article to
____ make you laugh.
__X__ give information.
____ persuade you to do something.

The author states some facts in the article. She also gives her opinion. Write **F** next to each sentence that is a fact. Write **O** next to each sentence that gives an opinion.

2. __F__ Add adults into the mix, and you come up with more than 18 million Americans playing soccer.
3. __O__ First, I think there's the international appeal.
4. __F__ Though accidents may occur, body contact isn't supposed to be part of the game.
5. __O__ And finally, I think there is the running factor.
6. Look back at the sentences you marked as opinions. What do you notice about them?
Answers will vary.

7. What is the main idea of paragraph 5?
____ Soccer is only for boys, just like other sports.
__✓__ Soccer is a good sport for both boys and girls.
____ Soccer has caught on with girls.

8. Why is soccer less expensive than some other sports?
You don't need a lot of equipment.

9. Look at the focus question under the title. What do you think its purpose is?
Possible answer: It tells you something to look for or think about as you read.

10. Have you ever played soccer? If so, tell about your experience. If not, explain why you would or would not like to try it.
Answers will vary.

39

1. Do you think Sharla, Tess, and Lee will be able to work together? Write why or why not.
Answers will vary.

2. Think of times when you worked with classmates on projects. Was it hard or easy? Explain.
Answers will vary.

3. Would you say that you are more like Sharla—full of ideas—or more like Lee—eager to stop talking and get to work? Write why.
Answers will vary.

4. Does the teacher who is writing the journal seem thoughtful or worn out? Write why you think so.
Answers will vary.

5. At the end of the first paragraph, the teacher says, "I knew something was going to blow up, and it wasn't the volcano." What does she mean?
Possible answer: She knows that the girls may end up having a fight.

6. From whose point of view is this selection told?
____ Sharla ____ Lee __✓__ the teacher

7. What do you predict will happen next in the story?
Answers will vary.

8. If you wrote a journal entry, what would you write about?
Answers will vary.

41

Answer Key

This story is written in the form of a journal entry. The person who is writing uses *I* to refer to herself. She is the **narrator**, or the person telling the story.

1. Find a sentence that tells you that the narrator actually took part in the action of the story. Write the sentence here.
   Answers will vary.
2. The narrator, Sharla, disagreed with Lee about
   whether to make the sides of the volcano smooth or rough.
3. Sharla was upset because
   she thought it was unfair to have to stay inside at recess.
4. Did you expect this journal to be written by Mrs. Holt, the teacher? Why or why not?
   Answers will vary.
5. Why did the girls decide to make a village around the base?
   Tess could do something without touching the volcano paste.
6. Which of these words best describes Sharla's attitude toward the other two girls?
   ✓ impatient ___ understanding ___ comforting
7. Explain how the picture adds to your understanding of the story.
   Possible answer: I can get an idea of what the volcano will look like. I can see that Tess is not really helping.
8. Write **C** next to the sentence below that is the cause. Write **E** next to the sentence that is the effect.
   C The girls didn't make much progress on their volcano.
   E Mrs. Holt made the girls stay in at recess.

43

1. In most stories, the characters have a problem. What problem do the characters in this story have?
   They disagreed about how to finish their project.
2. What caused Mrs. Holt to call the girls up to her desk?
   They weren't done with their project.
3. What is Tess's idea?
   X to show flowing lava
   ___ to make both sides smooth
   ___ to make the village larger
4. What is the result of Tess's idea?
   The girls agree to make one side smooth and one side rough. Sharla and Lee can both get what they want.
5. Where in the story do we learn that the teacher, Mrs. Holt, knows the girls are not getting along?
   In paragraph 5, it says, "knowing perfectly well that there was a problem."
6. What is the main difference in the way this story is written, compared to the other two about the same characters?
   ___ This story is told from Lee's point of view.
   ___ Sharla is not a character in this story.
   ✓ It is not written as a journal entry.
7. How do you think Mrs. Holt feels about the girls solving their own problem? Explain.
   Answers will vary.
8. What is the setting for this story?
   a school classroom
9. The girls learned how to build a volcano by doing this project. What else do you think they learned?
   Possible answer: They learned how to get along and work as a team.

45

1. This story is mostly about
   ___ becoming best friends after working together.
   X what the girls learned from their project.
   ___ how a teacher helped the girls get along.
2. How do the girls feel about their volcano project?
   They are proud of it.
3. When it is Lee's turn to speak, she feels
   X nervous.
   ___ happy.
   ___ cross.
4. Why did Sharla's face turn red when Mrs. Holt asked about how they completed their project?
   She was embarrassed.
5. What experiences have you had working with other people? Were there times when you didn't agree or get along? Write about it.
   Answers will vary.
6. When it is Tess's turn to speak, what does she tell about?
   a famous volcano and a town that got covered by mud and ash
7. Make a check mark next to the thing that happened first.
   ___ Mrs. Holt had a question.
   ✓ Lee said, "This is our volcano."
   ___ Mrs. Holt looked pleased.
8. If the girls had to work together again, how do you think they would do? Explain.
   Answers will vary.

47

In nonfiction writing, the author sometimes calls attention to words that the reader may not know. Those words appear in **bold** type. The author usually gives the meaning of the bold word in the same sentence.

Below are the bold words from the article. Write the meaning of each word.

1. molten melted
2. expand get bigger
3. fissures cracks
4. active experience eruptions
5. dormant inactive

Write **F** next to each sentence that is a fact. Write **O** next to each sentence that is an opinion.

6. O Volcanic eruptions are one of the most striking natural events.
7. O A volcanic eruption is more frightening than a hurricane.
8. F Volcanoes are located in many places in the world.
9. What does the illustration show?
   the inside of a volcano
10. Trace with your finger the path that magma would take from under Earth's crust to the surface. Describe the path in your own words.
    Answers will vary.
11. Write **C** next to the sentence below that is the cause. Write **E** next to the sentence that is the effect.
    E Parts of Earth's crust open up.
    C The molten rock gets very hot and expands.
12. What are scientists who study volcanoes called?
    volcanologists

49

Answer Key

Write the best word to complete each sentence below.

1. The students were especially **noisy** on Monday morning. (noisy, quiet, confused)
2. Miss Eller wrote the topic on the **board**. (notebook, list, board)
3. The teacher waved her **arms** all around. (ruler, book, arms)
4. Zach was only **kidding** about the grasshopper's knees. (wondering, kidding, thinking)
5. What do Miss Eller's students do as they begin their day? Find five details from the story and list them in order.
   empty backpacks, sign in, morning math problems, Morning Meeting, weather chart
6. What do you think will happen after lunch, when the students meet to talk about their new unit?
   Answers will vary.
7. What kind of decision do the students need to make?
   They need to choose a topic about the natural world.
8. Why does Miss Eller tell Kayla that Alaska might not be the best topic?
   It is too big.
9. According to Miss Eller, what does the natural world include?
   everything around us, and everything around people all over the world
10. Is this story realistic? Why or why not?
    Yes, the details are all things that could happen in real life.

51

1. Which of the students' ideas do you like best? Write why.
   Answers will vary.
2. Write **R** next to the sentences that tell about what Miss Eller's students could do for their study of the natural world. Write **M** next to the sentences that are about made-up things.
   M Isaac goes to the South Pole.
   R Tasha collects seeds.
   R Justin sets up a bird feeder.
   M Megan climbs the Alps.
3. What does this sentence from the story tell you about Miss Eller?
   "Miss Eller's quiet presence at the meeting rug was a signal for everyone to settle down and join her."
   Answers will vary.
4. Look for another sentence that tells you something about Miss Eller. What does it tell you?
   Answers will vary.
5. Why does Andy narrow down his topic?
   There are too many kinds of trees to study them all.
6. What is this story mostly about?
   ____ the natural world
   ____ how Miss Eller gets her class to behave
   ✓ a class coming up with ideas for a new unit of study
7. What problem does Miss Eller have at the end of the story?
   She's worried about how the class will agree on what to study.
8. If you were the teacher, how would you solve the problem?
   Answers will vary.

53

1. This story is mostly about
   X solving a problem.
   ____ how to do research.
   ____ getting ready for school.
2. Why does Miss Eller let the students offer so many ideas?
   She wants them to help decide what they study.
3. Write in your own words what Miss Eller's solution is.
   Answers will vary.
4. What are the students supposed to do during their sales pitch?
   convince the class to choose their topic to study
5. Based on the story, do you think Miss Eller is a good teacher? Back up your answer with events from the story.
   Answers will vary.
6. Andy wants to study **redwoods**.
7. Tara wants to study **fuzzy animals**.
8. What does Enzo ask at the end of the story? Why does this make Miss Eller think that her idea was a success?
   "Can I give out plastic snakes to help convince people?" Possible answer: She can tell that the students are excited about her idea.

55

1. What four common characteristics do mammals have?
   warm blood, backbones, milk fed to babies, and hair or fur

In the article, the author showed some words in bold type. The meanings of those words are given as well. Find the meanings of the words, and write them here.

2. habitat **natural conditions**
3. insectivores **insect eaters**
4. rodents **gnawing animals**
5. carnivores **meat eaters**
6. Hoofed animals are named for the kind of **feet** they have.
7. Give one example of each kind of forest dweller.
   Possible answers:
   insect eaters: **moles** gnawing animals: **beavers**
   hare-like animals: **rabbits** meat eaters: **coyotes**
   hoofed animals: **moose**
8. Why do you think a forest is a good habitat for many different kinds of mammals?
   Possible answer: There are lots of trees to provide shelter.
9. Think about what you know about mammals. Name two kinds of mammals that are not mentioned in the article. **Possible answers:**
   dogs and **dolphins**
10. **Meat eaters eat smaller mammals, such as rabbits, mice, and moles.** Is this sentence a fact or an opinion?
    a fact

57

Answer Key

The author of this article chose to share her own point of view. Find a sentence in which the author uses the word *I*. What idea is the author sharing in that sentence?

1. The sentence begins with
   Answers will vary.
   The author is saying Answers will vary.
2. Do you think the author likes snakes, dislikes snakes, or is neutral? Write a sentence from the article that supports your answer.
   Answers will vary.

Write **F** next to each sentence that is a fact. Write **O** next to each sentence that is an opinion.

3. O People dislike snakes because they have no legs.
4. F Snakes control the rodent population.
5. O Not meeting many snakes is a good thing.
6. Name one difference between mammals and reptiles.
   Possible answer: Mammals are warm-blooded, and reptiles are cold-blooded.
7. What is one way in which snakes are useful?
   They help control the rodent population.
8. What is the main idea of paragraph 4?
   ___ If you get bitten by a poisonous snake, seek medical help.
   ✓ Some snakes are poisonous, but that's not a good reason to dislike all snakes.
   ___ Poisonous snakes are very vicious.
9. Tell how you feel about snakes and why.
   Answers will vary.

59

1. To see a redwood tree, you have to go to Oregon or California.
2. Why do redwoods grow there?
   They need moisture from the ocean.
3. What might happen if someone tried to grow a redwood tree in Kansas or Missouri, for example?
   Answers will vary.
4. What do you think is most special about redwood trees? Write why.
   Answers will vary.
5. Why do you think the author chose to use questions for the headings?
   Answers will vary.
6. If you want to find out what conditions redwoods need to grow, under which heading would you look?
   Why do redwoods grow there?
7. If you wonder what the big deal is about redwoods, under which heading should you look?
   What's special about redwoods?
8. What three objects are shown in the diagram?
   a building, a tree, and a van
9. What is the author's purpose for writing this selection?
   ___ to entertain
   ___ persuade
   ✓ to inform
10. About how long can a redwood live?
    as long as 2,000 years

61

Complete each sentence with the correct word.

author	dialogue	narrator

1. When characters speak, their words make up the story's dialogue.
2. The person who wrote the story is the author.
3. Within the story, the person or character who tells the story is the narrator.
4. In most stories, the main character has a problem. Miss Eller's problem is that she needs to find a topic that will make everyone happy.
5. Look at the illustration. What did Miss Eller's students do during their study of redwood forests?
   Answers will vary.
6. Where did Miss Eller get the idea of how to solve the problem?
   She saw a poster of a woodland scene on the wall.
7. How do you think Miss Eller's class feels about the project?
   ✓ excited
   ___ worried
   ___ upset
8. The last paragraph says that the classroom had been transformed. What does this mean?
   Possible answer: It has been changed to look like something else.
9. Write **C** next to the sentence below that is the cause. Write **E** next to the sentence that is the effect.
   E Students raise their hands to answer the question.
   C Miss Eller asks what lives in a redwood forest.

63

In a tall tale, the author uses details that can't possibly be true to make the story funny. This is called **exaggeration**. Exaggeration is what makes a tall tale a tall tale.

1. Caleb, the narrator, tells us that the hamster has lived for 24 years. That is an exaggeration. Find another exaggeration in the story.
   Answers will vary.
2. Look at what you wrote for question 1. Why or how is it an exaggeration?
   Answers will vary.
3. What was the author's purpose in writing this story?
   to entertain or amuse
4. Do you think this story is realistic or a fantasy? Explain why.
   a fantasy; Possible answer: Many things that happen in the story could not happen in real life.
5. **Personification** means giving human characteristics to an animal or a thing. Give two examples of how the author personifies Felix.
   Possible answers: Felix can talk and write his own songs.
6. In the story, how does Felix make electricity for Caleb's family?
   by running on his wheel
7. **Felix is a musical hamster.** Find a line from the story to support this statement.
   Possible answer: I would see Felix tapping his little claws against the bars of the cage.

65

Answer Key

1. What do you know about taking care of a pet? How is taking care of a hamster the same or different from taking care of other kinds of pets?
   Answers will vary.
2. In the wild, hamsters sleep during the day and gather food during the night. Pet hamsters tend to follow the same schedule. If someone is thinking of getting a hamster, why is this important information to know?
   Answers will vary.

The author forgot to include headings in the article. Write where each heading should go.

3. **Equipment** should go before the third paragraph.
4. **Feeding Time** should go before the fifth paragraph.
5. **Choosing a Pet** should go before the second paragraph.
6. List the equipment you'll need to buy for your hamster.
   a cage, bedding, nesting material, an exercise wheel, a water bottle, a food dish, and food
7. The cage is the most expensive thing you will need to purchase.
8. What are some examples of good treats for a hamster?
   carrots, raisins, cheese, acorns
9. After reading this article, would you like to own a hamster? Why or why not?
   Answers will vary.

67

1. The story gives details about Frederick and the world in which he lives. Number these details in the order in which the story gives them.
   2 Noise had been a problem.
   5 Frederick liked his job.
   4 Frederick is a skyway sweeper.
   1 The skyway floors are padded.
   3 People stayed inside all the time.
   6 Frederick had never stepped on the ground.
2. As the story gives details, several sounds are mentioned. What are they?
   the swish of a broom, the sound of a footstep
3. Which of these best describes the story?
   ___ realistic fiction
   ___ a fairy tale
   ✓ science fiction
4. Write **C** next to the sentence below that is the cause. Write **E** next to the sentence that is the effect.
   C Noise had become a big issue.
   E Plastorub was put down everywhere, and the noise died down.
5. What does Frederick like about his job?
   He liked to see how things changed, and he liked the view.
6. What is the setting for this story?
   skyways in a city
7. Would you like to live in a world of skyways, like Frederick does? Explain.
   Answers will vary.

69

1. Write **R** next to the sentences that tell about something real. Write **M** next to the sentences that are about made-up things.
   M People do not know what dirt feels like.
   M The whole world is covered up with buildings.
   R People grow vegetables in gardens.
   M People stay indoors and never have to go outside.

In some stories, the problem is obvious. For example, maybe the character breaks an arm and has to learn how to write with the other hand, or something like that. In this story, the problem is not as obvious.

2. What problem does this character have?
   He has never felt real dirt and wonders what it's like.
3. According to the story, what is the word *sirt* supposed to make people think of?
   soil and dirt
4. In the story, how did all the real dirt get used up?
   There were too many people to feed and too many buildings covering up the ground.
5. How could you describe Frederick?
   ___ lazy
   ✓ a hard worker
   ___ hilarious
6. What effect does water have on sirt?
   It doesn't change it at all.
7. Reread the last paragraph. What do you predict will happen next?
   Possible answer: Frederick might try to find some real dirt.
8. In what time period do you think this story takes place? Why?
   Possible answer: the future; There is no dirt left, there are too many people, and people live in skyways.

71

Nonfiction articles and books sometimes have words in bold type. The author is pointing out a new or important word. Find the two bold words in the article. Then, look nearby for their meanings. Write them here.

1. Bold word: fragments
   Meaning: tiny pieces
2. Bold word: humus
   Meaning: a dark, slightly sticky substance that helps plants grow
3. What three things make up the soil?
   minerals, remains of dead plants and animals, and living organisms
4. When was the last time you dug in the soil? What did you see there?
   Answers will vary.
5. Now, look at the picture on page 72. What do you see there?
   Answers will vary.
6. How does this compare with what you saw when you dug in the soil yourself?
   Answers will vary.
7. How thick is the soil in most of North America?
   6 to 10 inches
8. What organisms help break down the dead material?
   bacteria, fungi, earthworms, and insects
9. Write **T** for **true** or **F** for **false** next to each statement below.
   T Not everyone has the same definition of dirt and soil.
   T Minerals come from rocks that have been broken into fragments.
   F Soil does not contain any living things.
   F Humus is harmful to plants.

73

Answer Key

1. Where does this story take place?
Answers will vary.
2. What is Frederick's dream?
to touch the ground, feel the dirt
3. What is Frederick's secret?
He is growing fruits and vegetables in real dirt.
4. Is it easy or difficult for Frederick to find a patch of dirt?
difficult
5. Why does Frederick receive an award?
for growing outstanding fruits and vegetables
6. The story doesn't tell us what happens after Frederick fills his shoes with dirt. What details from the story help you figure it out?
He wins an award for his fruits and vegetables. The newspaper headline wonders what his secret is.
7. Write two words to describe how Frederick feels when he finds real dirt.
Possible answer: joyful excited

75

1. The author's purpose was probably to
_____ entertain.
__X__ give information.
_____ persuade.
2. Improvements in elevator design made it possible to build taller buildings because Answers will vary.
3. What ideas did William Jenney have that changed how tall buildings could be?
He had the idea of using a steel frame with a thin "skin."
4. Is this article fiction or nonfiction?
nonfiction
5. How tall was Jenney's first tall building?
10 stories high
6. Write **C** next to the sentence below that is the cause. Write **E** next to the sentence that is the effect.
__E__ Buildings could be made taller.
__C__ Elevator design improved.
7. In paragraph 5, the article says that spires are included. Look up *spire* in a dictionary. Write the definition below.
Possible answer: spire: a sharp, pointed roof, like a steeple

77

1. This story is mostly about
__X__ two boys trying to do a magic trick.
_____ a boy teaching another boy a magic trick.
_____ how to do a magic trick.
2. Josh got wet because the flower vase tipped and spilled
3. Why was Josh under the table?
to pull the flower vase down; to make the flowers disappear
4. Write **C** next to the sentence below that is the cause. Write **E** next to the sentence that is the effect.
__E__ The vase tipped and got Josh wet.
__C__ The bottom of the box got stuck.
5. Why were the boys so excited about the old table they found?
It was perfect for doing magic tricks because of the hole.
6. Doing magic is (easier, (harder)) than the boys had expected.
7. Gary thinks that he and Josh need real things, so he tells Josh to go get a real rabbit.
8. Read the sentences below. Write **F** next to sentences that are facts and **O** next to sentences that are opinions.
__F__ Gary held his breath.
__O__ The boys should use real flowers.
__O__ Being a magician is hard work.
__F__ Josh's hair was wet.
9. What do you think will happen next?
Answers will vary.

79

1. How was the magic trick supposed to work?
Josh would pull Wiggles down through the bottom of the box.
2. What actually happened?
Wiggles actually got out without the boys noticing.

Write the best word to complete each sentence below.

3. They should have thought of Wiggles __sooner__. (brighter, sooner, calmer)
4. The magic words made the boys __laugh__ so hard. (laugh, lame, learn)
5. It made Gary feel like a real magician when he __waved__ his arms. (waved, cried, tapped)
6. The boys couldn't __believe__ Wiggles was gone. (agree, scramble, believe)
7. Write **R** next to the sentences that tell about something real. Write **M** next to the sentences that are about made-up things.
__R__ Rabbits eat lettuce.
__M__ Rabbits disappear and reappear.
__R__ Magicians say magic words.
8. In the story, who is the magician, and who is the assistant?
Gary is the magician, and Josh is the assistant.
9. Do you think the boys were surprised that Wiggles was actually gone? Why or why not?
Answers will vary.
10. Which words best describe the boys?
__✓__ good-natured
_____ sneaky
_____ irritated
11. What do you think will happen next in the story?
Answers will vary.

81

Answer Key

1. The author wrote this article to
   ______ persuade.
   ______ make you laugh.
   __X__ give you information.

Write **F** next to each sentence that is a fact. Write **O** next to each sentence that is an opinion.

2. __F__ Harry Houdini died more than 75 years ago.
3. __F__ Houdini could escape from handcuffs.
4. __O__ Harry Houdini was the only "real" magician.
5. __O__ Houdini's magic tricks were wonderful.
6. The article gives details about Houdini and his life. Number the details in the order in which the author tells about them.
   __3__ He escaped from a straitjacket, hanging upside down.
   __1__ Houdini had his first magic shows when he was 17.
   __4__ Houdini exposed "fake" magicians.
   __2__ Houdini's magic tricks became more showy and daring.
7. Which of these old sayings would Houdini have agreed with?
   __✓__ Practice makes perfect.
   ______ You are what you eat.
   ______ A watched pot never boils.
8. **Houdini believed he had special powers and could talk to spirits.** Is this statement true or false?
   false

83

1. David Copperfield is an illusionist.
2. What did he start doing at age 12?
   performing magic
3. What was he doing by age 16?
   teaching college-level classes

Check all answers that are correct.

4. Which of these words do you think best describe Copperfield?
   ______ thoughtless
   ______ lazy
   __✓__ hard-working
   __✓__ talented
5. What do you think a magician could learn from Copperfield's collection of old magic books and equipment?
   Answers will vary.
6. If you were a magician or an illusionist, what kinds of tricks would you like to do?
   Answers will vary.
7. The headings below belong in this article. To which paragraph does each heading belong?
   Copperfield's Beginnings 2nd
   What Is an Illusion? 1st
   Saving Magic for the Future 4th
   Project Magic 3rd
8. In your own words, explain what an illusion is.
   Possible answer: An illusion is like a trick on the eyes or the senses.
9. The youngest person ever to be allowed to join the Society of American Magicians was David Copperfield
10. Why do you think Copperfield believes that his best work is Project Magic?
    Possible answer: It's something he has done that helps other people and makes a difference in their lives.

85

1. Number the sentences to show the order in which events happened in the story.
   __2__ Gary laughed about their magic words.
   __4__ The boys heard Josh's mom.
   __5__ The boys discovered Mom and Wiggles.
   __3__ The boys figured out how to say the words backward.
   __1__ Gary felt great because their trick worked.
   __6__ The boys tried to make Mom's flowers reappear.
2. What problem do the boys have in this story?
   They can't find Wiggles the rabbit.
3. What problem does Mom have?
   Wiggles has eaten her flowers.
4. How do the boys try to help Mom? Do you think it will work?
   They try to do a magic trick to make her flowers reappear.
5. Who does Wiggles belong to?
   Josh
6. Do you think Wiggles has escaped before? What details in the story helped you answer this question?
   Yes, because Josh's mom says, "Now how many times . . ." This sounds as though Wiggles has escaped and eaten flowers many times before.
7. Do you think the boys will continue working on their magic tricks? Why or why not?
   Answers will vary.

87

1. The children notice that the town of Rockville is quite small.
2. What three sights do the children see out the bus window? Write the parts of the sentences from the story that tell you.
   "This is a little town... tall, dry cornfields... a long gray wall"

The place where a story happens is the **setting**. An author might describe how a place looks, how it feels, or how it smells. The author of this story described the setting in the first paragraph. Answer these questions.

3. During what time of year does this story take place?
   October
4. What kind of day is it?
   windy
5. What detail tells you that it might be a little chilly?
   It is windy, and the children have jackets on.
6. How do the students feel about the field trip?
   ______ annoyed
   ______ worried
   __✓__ excited
7. Name one detail from the story that helped you answer question 6.
   Posible answer: The story says that the wind "added to their excitement."
8. Write **C** next to the sentence below that is the cause. Write **E** next to the sentence that is the effect.
   __E__ No one is really looking out the windows much.
   __C__ The students are playing a game.
9. What do you think might be behind the long wall?
   Answers will vary.

89

Answer Key

Write **T** if the sentence is true. Write **F** if the sentence is false.

1. __F__ The children saw a castle.
2. __F__ The wall was on only one side of the bus.
3. __T__ Jason had a book on the bus.
4. __F__ The walls surrounded a lake.
5. What does this story tell you about Jason? You may check more than one.
   __✓__ He likes to joke around.
   __✓__ He is interested in history.
   ____ He doesn't get along with Steven.
   ____ He has never been on a field trip before.
6. Do you think Jason is reading a fiction or nonfiction book? How can you tell?
   Possible answer: nonfiction; The title sounds like an information book, not a story.
7. What is the purpose of the long gray wall?
   to block highway noise from people in the neighborhood
8. Why do the children decide that there's probably not a lake on the other side of the walls?
   There aren't any lakes that big around, and the wall is on both sides of the highway.
9. What is the author's purpose for writing this story?
   to entertain
10. Mrs. Mason ______.
   __✓__ knows a lot about the area
   ____ is too busy to talk to the students
   ____ probably just moved to the area

91

1. The Great Wall of China was built
   ____ as a place for soldiers to live.
   __X__ to protect China.
   ____ to honor the emperors.

Write the best word to complete each sentence below.

2. It took hundreds of years to __**build**__ the Great Wall of China. (move, build, climb)
3. Peasants were poor __**people**__ who did not have farms. (people, emperors, walls)
4. Today, people may __**visit**__ the Great Wall and walk along it. (twist, visit, hear)
5. What does the map show?
   China, the city of Beijing, and the Great Wall
6. Based on the map, describe how the Great Wall might look from high above Earth.
   Answers will vary.

Write the correct abbreviation in each blank.

mi. ft.

7. If you are standing on the Great Wall, you could be about 25 __**ft.**__ above the ground.
8. The top of the wall was made 12 __**ft.**__ wide so soldiers and carts could travel along the wall.
9. If every curve of the wall is measured, it is 1,500 __**mi.**__ long.
10. If a straight line were drawn from one end of the wall to the other, the line would be 1,200 __**mi.**__ long.
11. **The Great Wall of China was built by a single emperor.** Is this true or false?
   false
12. Why do you think watchtowers and cannons were added along the wall?
   for extra protection
13. What else can you think of that is another great human feat?
   Possible answer: sending humans to the moon

93

1. This article is mostly about
   ____ Maya Ying Lin.
   ____ the Vietnam War.
   __X__ the Vietnam Veterans Memorial.
2. The wall was completed in
   1982.
3. How many names are on the wall?
   58,245
4. Why was the Vietnam Veterans Memorial built?
   to remember everyone who served in the Vietnam War
5. Look at the picture of the wall. Then, look back at the design requirements. Write how you think the wall meets one of those requirements.
   Answers will vary.
6. How is the wall different from most walls?
   It brings people together instead of separating them.
7. Do you think that holding a contest to find a design for the wall was a good idea? Why or why not?
   Answers will vary.
8. The author's purpose for writing this article is
   ____ to entertain.
   __✓__ to inform.
   ____ to persuade.
9. If you visited the Vietnam Veterans Memorial, how do you think you would feel?
   Answers will vary.

95

1. What kind of day is it?
   a windy day
2. What are the children going to learn about?
   how people farmed and lived in the 1860s
3. How is Luisa's clothing different from Mrs. Hoff's?
   Mrs. Hoff is in a long dress, apron, and a little cap. Luisa is in jeans, a shirt, jacket, and sneakers.
4. Have you ever been on a field trip? What kinds of things did you do?
   Answers will vary.
5. Why is Mrs. Hoff dressed in old-fashioned clothing?
   to help students see what life was like long ago
6. About how old is the farm?
   ____ 100 years old
   __✓__ 140 years old
   ____ 160 years old
7. Is this story realistic? Why or why not?
   Yes, everything in the story could happen in real life.
8. What is the setting for this story?
   Fairfield Farm
9. What do you think will happen next?
   Answers will vary.

97

Answer Key

1. In the barn, the students saw
 a man and some sheep.

In this story, the author uses **dialogue** to move the story along. For each piece of dialogue below, fill in the name of the character who said it. Then, write what the dialogue tells you about the character or the story.

2. "I was just checking to see how the wool was growing."
 Mr. Brown; He knows about wool and sheep.
3. "Does wool really grow?"
 a student; The student doesn't know about wool or sheep.
4. "I clipped these sheep just about down to the skin in spring."
 Mr. Brown; Mr. Brown is the one who clipped the sheep's wool.
5. Write **R** next to the sentences that tell about something real. Write **M** next to the sentences that are about made-up things.
 R Farmers raise sheep.
 R A sheep's coat is wool.
 M Sheep come in many bright colors, just like yarn.
6. Number the sentences to show the order in which wool is processed.
 3 Card the wool.
 6 Weave the wool.
 1 Clip the wool.
 5 Spin the wool.
 2 Wash the wool.
 4 Dye the wool.
7. Why is Mr. Brown's name funny to Luisa?
 Everything he's wearing is brown, so his outfit matches his name.
8. What material is Mr. Brown's clothes made of?
 wool
9. **Then, someone weaves it into cloth.** Is this statement a fact or an opinion?
 a fact

99

1. It's hot in the kitchen because
 the wood stove is heating up the room.
2. What does the woman mean when she says, "The stove is hungry"?
 She means that the fire is going out and she needs more wood to keep it going.
3. Is Steven eager to taste the bread? How can you tell?
 Yes; at first he likes the smell. At the end he thinks, "with pleasure."

Write **F** next to each sentence that is a fact. Write **O** next to each sentence that is an opinion.

4. F Some people still bake their own bread.
5. O Bread is best when baked in a wood stove.
6. O All bread smells good when it's baking.
7. Why did farm wives bake bread only once a week?
 It's a long process, and the kitchen gets very hot.
8. After they fill up the wood box, what will the students do next?
 ___ get back on the bus
 ___ start a fire
 ✓ sample the bread
9. On the farm in the 1860s, Saturday was baking day.
10. Have you ever baked something from scratch before? Tell about it.
 Answers will vary.

101

1. What did Evelyn Seeley do before she retired?
 She owned a bakery.
2. What does she do now that she's retired?
 She bakes bread.
3. Number the sentences to show the order of the steps in the bread recipe.
 3 Add eggs.
 6 Let rise.
 4 Add milk, flour, and salt.
 1 Put yeast in water.
 5 Add yeast.
 2 Cream butter and sugar.
4. What type of selection is this?
 ___ a biography
 ✓ a newspaper article
 ___ a short story

Recipes often use short forms, or **abbreviations**, of words. Look at the common recipe words in the box. Write each word next to the correct item from the recipe.

cups	package
Fahrenheit	tablespoons
minutes	teaspoons

5. 40–45 min. minutes
6. 6 T. butter tablespoons
7. 350° F Fahrenheit
8. 3 c. flour cups
9. 1 pkg. dry yeast package
10. $1\frac{1}{4}$ tsp. salt teaspoons
11. Does the photo add anything to the article? Explain.
 Answers will vary.
12. Why does Seeley think she'll never run out of recipes now?
 Possible answer: She can look up new recipes on her computer.
13. Who runs Seeley's bakery today?
 her grown-up children

103

1. This story is mostly about
 ___ what the students learned on their field trip.
 X what the students liked best about the field trip.
 ___ how much Jason liked the geese.
2. What is Luisa's favorite part about the farm?
 the sheep
3. Which student seems unsure about his favorite part?
 Steven
4. How can you tell?
 First, he says the geese were his favorite, then the sheep, and then he says the bread was perfect.
5. Would you say that Steven is hard to please or easy to please? Explain.
 Answers will vary.
6. Where are the characters when they have this conversation?
 ___ in the barn
 ___ in the kitchen
 X on the bus
 ___ outside
7. Write **first**, **next**, and **last** to tell in what order the events below happened.
 last Steven had a dreamy look on his face.
 first Steven and Jason got on the bus.
 next Mrs. Mason said she liked the bread best.
8. Do you think Mrs. Mason really wanted to curl up in the pen with the sheep? Why or why not?
 Possible answer: No, she was just trying to tell how cozy she thought the sheep looked.

105

Answer Key

Write the best word to complete each sentence below.

1. Up ahead, the line of cars went around a **curve**. (curve, ledge, movement)
2. Jason was worried about the bus being **late**. (hard, late, extra)
3. Steven wanted to **count** the cars. (spin, read, count)
4. Have you ever been stuck in traffic? Write about how it felt.
   Answers will vary.
5. What might cause a traffic jam? List as many reasons as you can.
   Answers will vary.
6. How do you think the bus driver feels about the traffic jam?
   ____ amused
   ____ joyful
   ✓ frustrated
7. If the bus is late, what will the bus driver do?
   radio the school to let them know
8. Write **C** next to the sentence below that is the cause. Write **E** next to the sentence that is the effect.
   C Lots of cars are on the highway at the same time.
   E The cars are causing a traffic jam.

107

1. What kinds of things do we count? List two examples from the article.
   Ex.: inches of rain, students, government spending, voters, traffic accidents, etc.
2. What do we learn from counting things?
   Ex.: to see how things need to change or how things are changing
3. How do you think the information shown in this graph affects you and your community?
   Answers will vary.
4. What can the number of traffic accidents tell us?
   where new stop signs and lights should go
5. How many years does this chart cover?
   40 years
6. Why is the title of the chart important?
   It tells you what the chart shows.

Use the bar graph to answer these questions.

7. For each year, which is greater, the population or the number of cars?
   the population
8. If you want population data for 1950, would this graph help you? How can you tell?
   No. The title says that the graph includes data only for 1960–2000.
9. What was the population of the United States in 1970?
   about 203.2 million, or just over 200 million
10. How many cars were there in 1990?
    about 133.7 million, or about 130 million

109

1. Tatsu is sitting in the shade on the front steps because
   it is a very hot day.
2. Tatsu titles her drawing "Heat" because
   the sun is what is making her so hot.
3. Write **R** next to the sentences that tell about something real. Write **M** next to the sentences that are about made-up things.
   M A person can make shade by drawing a picture of it.
   M A person can draw a picture of heat.
   R A person can draw a picture of the sun.

The **narrator** is the person who tells a story. Answer these questions.

4. Because the narrator is also a character, she uses the words *I* and *me* to tell her story. Find a place in the story where one of these words is used. Write the sentence here.
   Answers will vary.
5. Where in the story do you discover what the narrator's name is?
   When her brother asks her a question.
6. Do you think Tatsu and Fujio live in the city, in the country, or in a small town? Why?
   a city; Possible answer: They live in an apartment building. The picture looks like a city, with lots of concrete.
7. From whose point of view is the story told?
   ✓ Tatsu's ____ Fujio's ____ Not enough information is given.
8. The author uses lots of descriptions to tell how hot it is. List three details from the story that help you imagine the heat.
   Possible answers: Everything feels hot and sticky, including my own skin; I feel like the glass greenhouse at the city park; I can count on the fingers of one hand the number of leaves moving in the breeze.
9. What do you like to do on a super hot summer day?
   Answers will vary.

111

1. Why do Mario and Katie choose to draw pictures of cool water and a snow bank?
   because it helps them think about being cool on a hot day
2. Why does Tatsu cross out her own picture of the sun?
   She thinks it might be making things feel hotter.
3. Which word best describes the group of friends?
   ____ energetic
   ✓ creative
   ____ anxious
4. Mario doesn't use words to ask Fujio what he drew. How does he ask instead?
   He raises his eyebrows.
5. What is the author's purpose in writing this story?
   ____ to teach ____ to persuade ✓ to entertain
6. Why is the story titled "Wishes on the Sidewalk"?
   Possible answer: The kids draw pictures on the sidewalk of things they are wishing for.
7. Do you think that thinking about cool things can help a person cool down? Write why or why not.
   Answers will vary.
8. Can you remember a hot day? How did it feel? Describe it so that someone else can imagine it easily.
   Answers will vary.

113

Answer Key

1. This article is mostly about
   _____ animals that lived thousands of years ago.
   __X__ early cave art.
   _____ how early people survived.
2. What did early cave artists use for paint?
   animal fat mixed with dirt or berries
3. Where did early artists make their drawings?
   on walls deep inside caves
4. Early cave art has been found in more than __130__ caves.
5. How do you like the cave art shown on this page? How is it the same or different from other drawings you have seen of mammoths?
   Answers will vary.
6. Who is the author addressing, or talking to, in this article?
   _____ the reader
   __✓__ the people who made the cave paintings
   _____ artists of today
7. Why is this an unusual way to write the article?
   Possible answer: Those people have been dead for thousands of years. They are not reading the article.
8. Most of the cave drawings have been found in __France__ and __England__.
9. What is the main idea of paragraph 4?
   People drew what they saw around them.
10. About how many years ago were the cave paintings made?
    about 17,000 years

115

1. Would you like to have a mural in your home? Write why or why not.
   Answers will vary.
2. Do you think the author wrote this article to make you laugh, give you information, or persuade you to do something?
   to give information
3. The author included some bold words in the article. He wanted readers to learn those words, so he included their meanings nearby. Find one of the words and look for its meaning. Write the word and its meaning here.
   Answer should site murals, myths, or mosaic, along with its meaning from the article.

Write the best word to complete each sentence below.

4. I would like a __picture__ of a garden on my wall.
   (jacket, picture, notebook)
5. The bread in the Roman __bakery__ mural looks yummy.
   (bakery, crown, sticky)
6. Would you like to use a million tiny __pieces__ to make a mosaic?
   (pieces, motions, signs)
7. Write **T** for **true** or **F** for **false** next to each statement below.
   __T__ Romans created sculptures on the sides of their buildings.
   __F__ A mosaic is carved into a stone wall.
   __F__ Murals do not tell us much about the ancient Romans.
   __T__ Myths are traditional stories.
8. What is paragraph 4 mostly about?
   Roman murals and what they showed
9. What kind of artwork hangs on the walls of your home? What does it say about your family?
   Answers will vary.

117

1. The members of Lucy's family are
   her father, mother, and brother.
2. What is Lucy's real name?
   Lucinda
3. Where does Lucy's pen pal live? How do you know?
   In the Dominican Republic; Lucy wonders whether the water in North Carolina had come from there.
4. What details do we learn about Lucy from her letter?
   She has red hair; she is in third grade; she has two parents and a brother; she sings in a choir
5. What do you think will happen after Lucy finishes writing her letter?
   Answers will vary.
6. How do Lucy's teacher and Isabel's teacher know each other?
   Their teachers used to be pen pals.
7. What makes Lucy feel closer to Isabel?
   She imagines that they have touched the same water.
8. What is paragraph 4 of Lucy's letter mostly about?
   her trip to the beach in South Carolina
9. If you had a pen pal, what important details would you share about yourself?
   Answers will vary.

119

1. What do all beaches have in common?
   They all have some kind of rock or stone material.
2. Why do beaches have stones or sand on them?
   The water, wind, rain, and frost break down rocks into smaller pieces.
3. What causes waves?
   wind
4. Why does the article mention a rug?
   The rug is an example of how a wave works.
5. This article has two sections. What are they titled?
   "The Beach" and "The Waves"
6. If you were especially interested in water, what section would you look under?
   The Waves
7. "They can nibble at your toes in the sand, or they can be loud and crashing and dangerous." What is the author describing?
   the waves
8. What forces work together to break down rock into smaller pieces?
   waves, wind, rain, and frost
9. Is this selection fiction or nonfiction?
   nonfiction
10. Have you ever been to the beach? If so, describe it. If not, tell about what kind of beach you would like to visit.
    Answers will vary.

121

Answer Key

Isabel wrote a friendly letter to her pen pal. She began the letter with "Dear Lucy." That is the **greeting**. She ended her letter with "Your pen pal, Isabel." That is the **closing** of the letter.

1. Suppose you are writing a letter. Write the greeting of your letter here. Remember to put a comma after your greeting.
   Ex.: Dear Grandma,
2. Now, write the closing of your letter. Note that there is a comma between the closing words and your name.
   Ex.: Love, Simon

Write **T** if the sentence is **true**. Write **F** if the sentence is **false**.

3. **F** Isabel is the oldest child in her family.
4. **F** Isabel's father makes his living by playing guitar.
5. **T** Isabel thinks her mother is a good cook.
6. **T** Isabel sometimes feels bossed around by her sisters.
7. Name three things that Isabel and Lucy have in common.
   Possible answers: They both have at least one sibling; Their fathers work with houses; They both enjoy the beach.
8. What does Isabel say Lucy should do the next time she sees the moon?
   She says that Lucy should think of Isabel and her mama dancing on the beach.
9. **The Dominican Republic is an island.** Is this true or false? How do you know?
   true; In paragraph 6, Isabel says, "on my island."
10. If you were writing a letter back to Isabel, what would you want to ask her about her life?
    Answers will vary.

123

1. The Dominican Republic is about as big as **Connecticut** and **Rhode Island** combined.
2. Which population is larger---the Dominican Republic's or Connecticut and Rhode Island's?
   the Dominican Republic's
3. What does the article say about the Dominican Republic's weather?
   It is tropical.
4. What do you know about the weather in Connecticut and Rhode Island? How would it compare to the Dominican Republic's weather?
   It would be colder in Connecticut and Rhode Island than it would be in the Dominican Republic.
5. If the author wanted to add this sentence to the article, under what heading should it go?
   Workers also harvest valuable lumber from the coastal forests.
   What Happens There?
6. If you need a quick reminder about the location of the island, under what heading should you look?
   Where Is It?

Look at the map to answer these questions.

7. Which city is the capital? How can you tell?
   Santo Domingo; It is marked with a star.
8. What city is farther north than the others?
   Santiago
9. What country lies to the west of the Dominican Republic?
   Haiti
10. Why is February a good time to visit the Dominican Republic?
    You can go to Carnival.

125

1. Lucy is excited because **she just got a letter from her pen pal**.
2. Lucy's mother is just returning from **grocery shopping**.
3. Does Lucy seem helpful or selfish in this story? Give reasons for your answer.
   Answers will vary.

Lucy notices that she and her pen pal, Isabel, are alike in some ways and different in others. Help her compare. Write what is the same about both girls in the space provided. Then, write what is different about each girl.

Lucy	Both	Isabel
has one younger brother	like to go to beach; dads are in house-building business; mothers are great cooks	has four older sisters

4. Choose one piece of dialogue from the story, and write it on the line. Tell what the dialogue tells you about the character or the story.
   Possible answer: "Well, that's natural." Mom is reassuring and kind.
5. In paragraph 14, why does Mrs. Teeman look crushed?
   She thinks that Lucy thinks that she is not a good cook.
6. Write **C** next to the sentence below that is the cause. Write **E** next to the sentence that is the effect.
   C Lucy twirled around with a bunch of bananas for a partner.
   E Mrs. Teeman laughed at Lucy's excitement.
7. In paragraph 2, Mrs. Teeman says that Lucy won't have to camp out by the mailbox anymore. What does she mean?
   She means that Lucy won't have to spend so much time waiting by the mailbox.

127

1. Number the sentences to show the order in which things happened.
   3 Kyle gives Mom the phone message.
   4 Mom goes to school on Thursday.
   1 Mom goes out to mow the lawn.
   2 Kyle takes a phone call for Mom.
   5 Mrs. Essman asks Mom where the cake is.
2. Why does Mom take cookies to school on Thursday?
   She thought they were needed for a bake sale.
3. While he is talking on the phone, Kyle is also **doing his homework**.
4. What is the setting for this story?
   Kyle's kitchen
5. What type of story is this?
   ✓ realistic fiction ____ science fiction ____ a tall tale
6. In paragraph 7, the author says that Mom is getting a little prickly. What does this mean?
   Possible answer: She is starting to sound irritated.
7. What do you think Kyle will do the next time he answers the phone? Why?
   Possible answer: He will take a message and give it to his mom. He learned from his mistake.
8. Do you think it was fair for Kyle's mom to be frustrated with him? Explain.
   Answers will vary.

129

Answer Key

1. What important parts of a phone message did Kyle forget the other day?
   All four parts—name, number, write it down, and deliver the message
2. Look at the illustration. What do you think Mom is saying? Write the dialogue.
   Answers will vary.
3. Why is Mom talking to the boys as though they are four years old?
   Possible answer: She wants to be very clear with them about phone manners.
4. Look at the picture of Kyle and Anthony. What do you learn about the boys from the picture that isn't in the story?
   They are probably twins.
5. How will the boys be tested?
   They will be tested each time the phone rings.
6. Do you think Mom's phone class will be a success? Why or why not?
   Answers will vary.

You have just attended the Phone Manners from Mom class. How should you respond to these telephone situations?

7. The phone rings. You answer it by saying, "**Hello. (Last Name) residence. This is (First Name) speaking.**"
8. Your dad is reading a book on the porch. The phone rings and the person says, "May I speak to your father?" What do you say?
   Yes you may. May I ask who is calling, please?
9. Your mom is washing her hair and can't come to the phone, so you must take a message. What are the four important parts of a phone message?
   name, number, write it down, deliver the message

131

1. What surprised Kyle and Anthony about Uncle Dale's phone conversation?
   ____ the fact that he had even answered the phone
   __X__ the way he spoke
   ____ the length of the conversation
2. Number the sentences to show the order in which events happened.
   __6__ Uncle Dale gets a lesson on how to take phone messages.
   __2__ Uncle Dale arrives.
   __4__ Uncle Dale answers the phone.
   __1__ Kyle takes a phone message.
   __5__ Mom enters the kitchen.
   __3__ Kyle greets Uncle Dale.
3. Why does Uncle Dale's face look a little pained in paragraph 11?
   Possible answer: He realizes that he made a mistake.
4. Why are Kyle and Anthony not supposed to say "yeah" on the phone?
   It is not good manners.
5. How are Uncle Dale and Mom related to each other?
   They are brother and sister.
6. Do you think that Uncle Dale will use better phone manners in the future? Explain.
   Answers will vary.

133

1. The article says it's not your voice, but **sound waves** made by your voice, that enter the telephone's microphone.
2. When the current in a telephone wire is flowing smoothly, what does the person on the other end hear?
   nothing
3. When sound waves interrupt the flow of current, what does the person on the other end hear?
   the speaker's voice
4. How long ago did people know that sound could travel along a wire?
   almost 400 years ago
5. How long ago did Alexander Graham Bell invent the telephone?
   about 130 years ago

Write **F** next to each sentence that is a fact. Write **O** next to each sentence that is an opinion.

6. __F__ Sound waves travel along a wire with the help of an electrical current.
7. __O__ The telephone is the most important invention of the last 200 years.
8. __O__ Without the telephone, modern businesses would fail.
9. How does the computer know to connect you to the person you are trying to call?
   When you dial the person's phone number, that tells the computer to connect your phone to theirs.
10. **Telephones have been around for less than a hundred years.** Is this statement true or false?
    false
11. How do you and other members of your family use the telephone today?
    Answers will vary.
12. What would it be like if you had to get along without telephones? How else would you communicate?
    Answers will vary.

135

1. What clues tell you that the narrator is in bed? Write the words or phrases from the story.
   "snuggled under the covers"; "too close to sleep"
2. How do you know that having pancakes for breakfast must be a special thing?
   It says the smell of pancakes was not a normal smell.
3. The word that best describes this family is
   ____ rough.
   ____ noisy.
   __X__ pleasant.
4. What is the setting for this story?
   the narrator's kitchen
5. Write two things you know about the narrator of the story.
   Possible answers: She likes pancakes. She has a brother and a sister.
6. Why does the girl feel sorry for her younger brother?
   He is too little to eat pancakes.
7. Explain the title of the story, "Honey to the Rescue."
   Possible answer: The family is out of syrup, but they can still have pancakes because they have honey.
8. Why is the first sentence of the story ("*What's that smell?*") in italics?
   The narrator is thinking it, not saying it aloud.

137

Answer Key

1. List the reasons the author gives for making honey our national food.
   Honey lasts pretty much forever. Honey is sweet. The bees would like it. Honey is useful.
2. Do you think those are good reasons for naming honey as a national food? Write why or why not.
   Answers will vary.
3. Sometimes, an author has more than one purpose for writing. What two purposes do you think this author had for writing the honey article?
   X to entertain readers
   ___ to give an explanation of honey bees' lives
   X to persuade readers that honey is good
   ___ to describe how honey resists bacteria
4. This article is mostly about
   X how good honey is.
   ___ the food value of honey.

Write the best word to complete each sentence below.

5. It's amazing that the honey didn't spoil. (burst, spoil, mend)
6. I like to spread honey on hot toast. (spread, clap, handle)
7. As bees collect nectar, they also spread pollen. (collect, enter, change)
8. What would happen to flowers without bees and butterflies?
   They would not be able to exist anymore.
9. This article contains facts about bees and honey, but it also contains the author's opinion. Give one example of each. **Possible answers:**
   Fact: It wasn't moldy or rotten.
   Opinion: I think the bees would like it if we made honey our national food.
10. Name one way in which bees use the honey they make.
   They feed it to the larvae.

139

1. Write **R** next to two sentences that tell about real things.
   R Anyone can make up a song.
   R A song can be happy or sad.
   ___ The words of a song are always true.
2. Read the sentences below. Write **F** next to sentences that are facts and **O** next to sentences that are opinions.
   F Eliza raised her hand.
   O Well, that's a good question.
   O I guess that's not much different from us.
   F Mr. Hamlin let them think some more.
3. Choose one piece of dialogue from the story, and write it on the line. Tell what the dialogue tells you about the character or the story.
   Possible answer: "Hmm, well that's a good question." Mr. Hamlin is a good teacher. He encourages his students.
4. The students figure out that people like to make up songs about everyday things.
5. Earlier that day, Eliza says she sang a song about her socks.
6. Which word best describes Eliza?
   ✓ curious
   ___ sneaky
   ___ nervous
7. If you wrote a song, what everyday things could you put in it?
   Answers will vary.

141

1. What is the difference between a ballad and a folk song?
   A ballad is longer and usually tells a story. A folk song is shorter and tells of a feeling or experience.
2. Why do you suppose someone wrote "Farewell, Nancy"?
   A sailor was leaving his wife or girlfriend to go to sea.
3. Why do you think someone would make a song about saying good-bye?
   Answers will vary. Ex.: It might help someone say good-bye. It might help when "Nancy" is missing the sailor.
4. "When Johnny Comes Marching Home Again" is a well-known ballad. Even if you don't know the words, the title hints at the song's story. What do you think it is?
   Answers will vary but may mention a soldier coming home from war.
5. Write **T** for **true** or **F** for **false** next to each statement below.
   F People's feelings are very different today than they were long ago.
   T Most folk songs have been written recently.
   T Folk music can be about a number of different topics and emotions.
6. Why do you think people might write folk songs during wars?
   Answers will vary.
7. What two main emotions does the sailor have in "Farewell Nancy"?
   sadness and hope
8. Why do you think that we don't know who wrote most folk songs?
   Possible answer: They were written long ago and passed down through many people.

143

1. What do Grandma and Grandpa do for a living?
   They are farmers.
2. Do you think Grandma likes peanut butter? Why?
   Ex.: Yes, because she liked the sandwich Grandpa made.
3. Do you think you would like a peanut butter-bacon-banana sandwich?
   Answers will vary.
4. What do you think will happen next?
   Answers will vary.
5. Write **C** next to the sentence below that is the cause. Write **E** next to the sentence that is the effect.
   E Grandma helped out in the fields.
   C Grandpa broke his leg.
6. Where are Max and A.J. taking their picnic?
   to Grandpa, who is planting corn
7. What would Max and A.J. like to have for lunch better than anything else?
   peanut butter and jelly sandwiches
8. Why did Grandma eat the sandwich, even though it sounded awful to her?
   She didn't want to hurt Grandpa's feelings.

145

Answer Key

1. This article is mostly about
   __X__ Carver's work with peanuts.
   _____ Carver's fame as a scientist.
   _____ Carver's fight to get an education.
2. George Washington Carver lived from __1864__ until __1943__.
3. While in college, he studied __agriculture__, which is the study of __farming__.
4. Carver made hundreds of products from peanuts. List some that the article mentions.
   Answers will vary.
5. Which of the products seems the most interesting or the most unusual to you? Write why.
   Answers will vary.

Write **F** next to each sentence that is a fact. Write **O** next to each sentence that is an opinion.

6. __O__ Carver saved Southern farmers from ruining the land.
7. __F__ Planting peanuts after cotton keeps the soil healthy.
8. __O__ Carver is America's greatest black scientist.
9. Based on the article, it seems that the author _____ Carver.
   _____ dislikes
   __✓__ admires
   _____ ignores
10. Why is it a good idea to rotate crops, instead of planting the same thing over and over?
    It gives the soil chance to rest, and it produces healthier crops.
11. Reread the first line of paragraph 5. Do you feel that Carver made the right choices? Explain.
    Answers will vary.

147

Write the best word to complete each sentence below.

1. Stephanie and her mom look for a box in the __attic__.
   (attic, entrance, ending)
2. Stephanie was proud that she had __built__ her present.
   (waved, built, filled)
3. Stephanie was __curious__ about Mom's wrapping idea.
   (clever, crazy, curious)
4. Explain how Stephanie will make the wrapping paper.
   She will use stamps, sponges, and paints on plain brown paper.
5. Write two adjectives you could use to describe Stephanie. **Possible answers:**
   __creative__ and __thoughtful__
6. Look at the picture. Where do you think Stephanie and her mom are?
   _____ in the living room __✓__ in the garage _____ in Stephanie's room
7. From whose point of view is the story told?
   Stephanie's
8. Do you think Dad will like Stephanie's gift? Why or why not?
   Answers will vary.

149

1. The author used a numbered list for the instructions. Why do you think this was done?
   Answers will vary.
2. What other kinds of instructions, with numbered lists, have you seen?
   Answers will vary.
3. Number the sentences to show the order in which to complete the stamping project.
   __3__ Dip stamp into paint.
   __4__ Press stamp on paper.
   __1__ Put paint in plastic lids.
   __6__ Let dry.
   __2__ Lay out sheet of paper.
   __5__ Lift the stamp.
4. Why do the instructions say you should put small amounts of paint in plastic lids?
   So you can dip stamps easily.
5. What can you think of that you would like to decorate with stamps?
   Answers will vary.
6. Explain how you can make your own stamps.
   You can cut them out of fruits or vegetables, or you can use household items.
7. What is the author's purpose?
   __✓__ to instruct _____ to entertain _____ to persuade
8. Does this sound like a craft you would like to try? Why or why not?
   Answers will vary.

151

Notes

Notes

Notes